January Bible Study

James:
FAITH WORKS!

Joel C. Gregory

CONVENTION PRESS • NASHVILLE, TENNESSEE

Contents

Dewey Decimal Classification Number: 227.91
Subject Heading: Bible. N.T. James
Printed in the United States of America.

This book is the text for a course in the subject area Bible Study of the Church Study Course.

Target group: This book is designed for adults and is part of the Church Study Course offerings. The 1963 statement of "The Baptist Faith and Message" is the doctrinal guideline for the writer and editor.

A Word to Begin . . .

"The Letter of James has less about Jesus' life than any other New Testament letter. Yet, no other epistle reflects more of Jesus or contains as many echoes of His words." With this incisive observation, Joel Gregory highlights one of the unique features of the Letter of James.

The Letter of James has been called the most practical document in the New Testament. James's purpose was to give his readers directives for Christian living. He may have intended to challenge believers to a broader, deeper faith that was not content with mere verbal confession. James wrote to early Christians; however, today's believers still can profit from his strong exhortations.

Joel C. Gregory is pastor of Travis Avenue Baptist Church, Fort Worth, Texas. He is known widely as an exceptional preacher and Bible study leader. He has produced a warm, insightful, inspiring study of James.

This textbook may be used in personal or group study. In both uses, the Personal Learning Activities at the end of each chapter will help the learner to review the material that has been covered. In group study, the companion Study Guide will provide helpful resources for the teacher and the members. The *Teaching Guide for James: Faith Works!* will help the study leader direct the sessions. The *James: Faith Works! Teaching Resource Kit, 1987,* will provide teaching aids for the study. In this textbook, guidance for using Personal Learning Activities is in the section entitled "The Church Study Course" at the end of the book.

Also at the back of the book is a Church Study Course Credit Request (Form 725). On completion of this book, the pupil should mail in the completed form to the address that is indicated. Twice each year, up-to-date reports called "transcripts" will be sent to churches to distribute to members who take part in the Church Study Course.

Eli Landrum, Jr., editor

1
Tests of a Vital Faith

James 1:1-18

James—The Brother of Jesus

The first word of the Letter of James identifies the writer: "James" (1:1). In Hebrew, the name James is *Jacob*. At least three prominent followers of Jesus bore this name: James the son of Alphaeus; James the son of Zebedee; and James, the Lord's half brother. James the son of Alphaeus drops out of the biblical record so completely that he probably was too unimportant to get away with the simple designation that opens the letter. Herod Agrippa I beheaded James the son of Zebedee about AD 42-44 (Acts 12:2). Obviously, the man who wrote the Book of James was so well known that he only needed to use his first name. James the half brother of Jesus meets that qualification.

God sent His Son to a home. All of the daily difficulties and tedious chores of domestic life conditioned Christ's growth. James observed his older half brother's reaction to them all. One can guess James's thoughts as he watched Jesus wander the hillsides of Galilee, often meditating on the scroll of Isaiah. James witnessed the day when Jesus left their quiet home to walk to the Jordan River where John the Baptizer preached. What shock seized James when Jesus returned to preach in the synagogue at Nazareth and claimed to fulfill the words of Isaiah (Luke 4:16-21)? James's and others' verdict appears plainly in Mark 3:21. They thought Jesus was out of His mind. John recorded that Jesus' brothers half taunted Him, insinuating that a real prophet should show himself in Jerusalem (John 7:1-5). John clearly stated that Jesus' brothers did not believe in Him.

Do you have a family member who rejects Christ's claims? Perhaps you would be encouraged to know that Jesus' own brothers rejected Him at first. No record shows that His sisters ever placed their faith in Him as Savior and Lord. You have not failed just because your family does not believe. Jesus did not coerce James into belief.

How, then, did Jesus' unbelieving brother become the chief pastor of the church at Jerusalem and the leader of the first great church council? (See Acts 15.) The key seems to be an appearance to James by the risen Christ. Paul alone recorded that Jesus appeared to James for a special conversation (1 Cor. 15:7). For James, Jesus' resurrection transformed a mere brother into a glorious Lord.

James's transformation caused him to wait with the disciples in the upper room for the Holy Spirit's power (Acts 1:14). With the death of James the son of Zebedee about AD 42-44, James, Jesus' brother, became head of the Jerusalem church.

James—a Palestinian Jew

The Letter of James breathes the atmosphere of Palestinian Judaism. Even without the author's name, one could know that he lived in the Promised Land. For example, James wrote of the patient Palestinian farmer who waited for the early and late rains (Jas. 5:7). The early and late rains were characteristic of Palestine, not of Italy, Egypt, or Asia Minor. James the Jew wrote of "Abraham our father" (2:21), "Lord of sabaoth" (5:4, KJV), and assumed that his readers were familiar with Job, the prophets, and Jewish law. He even called the Christian place of worship a synagogue (2:2, Greek text)! God always uses the background of those whom He calls. So, James the Jew wrote his letter for those whom he knew best, Jewish Christians.

The Letter of James has less about Jesus' life than any other New Testament letter. Yet, no other epistle reflects more of Jesus or contains as many echoes of His words. For instance, James made at least fourteen allusions to Jesus' Sermon on the Mount. Each chapter of James has echoes of his half brother's great Sermon. If Jesus' words so saturated believers' conversations, what impact would they make?

An Early Letter

The Letter of James does not come with a postmark. How does one know when a letter like this was written? Suppose you went to a meeting one year that changed your life and the lives of those around you. If you wrote a Christmas letter to all of your friends that year, would you not describe that meeting, or at least mention it? Or, suppose that the city where you live was destroyed. You certainly would mention that in your letter. Similarly, in about AD 49-51 James presided over a meeting that changed the church. At the Jerusalem Council, Gentiles were freed from keeping the Jewish law in order to become Christians. In AD 70, James's city, Jerusalem, was wasted. Indeed, a strong tradition places James's death in AD 62. James's letter makes no reference either to the council or to the destruction of Jerusalem. Because of that, it may have been written sometime between AD 44 and 50. This would make the letter a rival for the honor of the oldest writing in the New Testament.

The Letter of James was not as quickly accepted as authoritative Scripture by the early church as were some other books. The first clear reference to the Book of James as Holy Scripture came from the theologian Origen of Alexandria in North Africa sometime after AD 231. By AD 393, however, the whole church had accepted the biblical authority of James. Later, Martin Luther disparaged the letter. He called it an epistle of straw because he thought that James disagreed with Paul's view of faith. Luther put the letter at the end of his German translation of the New Testament. Now, the book is where it belongs: in the midst of the great General Letters of the New Testament. Today, believers accept its authority as a God-breathed Word without error.

James—Brother and Servant

Today, writers sign their letters at the end. Often, readers look at the bottom of a letter first to see who wrote it. Ancient writers stated first who wrote the letter. James began his letter in this manner (1:1).

Note that James claimed no special title. He could have claimed botherhood with Jesus; yet, in humility, he made no mention of that tie. James did not claim his title as pastor of the Jerusalem church or even as an apostle. He simply was James, standing before his Lord without any earthly title. Every believer stands before Christ in this manner.

Indeed, the only thing that James wrote about himself was that he was a bondslave "of God and of the Lord Jesus Christ" (1:1). The only claim that he made was one of ownership by God in Christ. Like all believers, he was bought with a price (1 Cor. 6:20). The language that James used connected Christ with the God of the Old Testament. Such confession offers a unique testimony to Jesus. James shared the Nazareth home, the boyhood days, and the Galilean hills with Jesus. Yet, he confessed that his brother now was his Lord and deserved equal devotion with Jehovah God of the Old Testament.

God's Scattered People

God had not lost the address of His Old Covenant people. James sent the letter "to the twelve tribes which are scattered abroad" (1:1, KJV). He included as the recipients all Jews as well as Christian Jews.

Remember that the earliest Jewish believers had no sectarian name that separated them from other Jews. Many had not broken from the synagogue. At first, Jewish Christians maintained the hope that all of their fellow Jews would turn to Christ. James chose the strongest possible way to address all Jews. Gentiles read and profited by James's letter, but I feel that he wrote primarily to his Jewish brethren.

God's people usually have been scattered. Thus, James addressed the twelve scattered tribes. By the time James wrote, as many as 4,000,000 Jews were scattered in the Roman world. The different groups of people who listened to Peter's sermon in Acts 2 suggests how dispersed the Jews were. In almost every distant city, Paul found a synagogue. Strabo, a geographer who was contemporary with Jesus, exclaimed: "It is hard to find a spot in the whole world which is not occupied and dominated by the Jews."[1] They were Jews of the Diaspora or Dispersion.

Only a persevering postman could have carried James's letter to all the scattered Jews! This letter probably addressed a particular group of the Diaspora. Those immediately north in Syria or those in the oldest resettlements in Mesopotamia likely received this general letter. Jewish Christians who were driven out after Stephen's death resettled in these areas. (See Acts 8:1; 11:19.) (Some interpreters hold that the phrase "the twelve tribes in the Dispersion" [1:1] refers to the true people of God everywhere.)

Contemporary Christians need to recover the concept of being scattered. In New Testament times, God purposely scattered the Jews as He scattered seed for gospel soil. Too often, Christians have gathered together in safe enclaves rather than to disperse to witness to the world. Today, holy huddles need to break up into world witnesses.

Churches have built their own gymnasiums, schools, and intricate social structures. While none of these is wrong in itself, all of them together can keep believers from being scattered as salt and light in a rotting and darkened world. One minister received an advertisement for a Christian subdivision in which only born again people could live within its walls. That conjures up the image of Christian grocery stores where only Christians may shop for consecrated corn flakes, justified jelly, and sacred sauerkraut! Christians must risk contact with a spiritually sick world's festering need. In James's day, God scattered His people throughout the Roman Empire.

Testing Times (1:2-4)

How do people face life's tests? God's providence gives believers daily quizzes and periodic final examinations in Christian living. Some persons react to life's tests with denial. They say: *This is not happening to me.* Others react with escape; they turn to marijuana, cocaine, or a promiscuous one-night stand. Still others respond to trials with a shallow, humanistic optimism. In a tiny church where members quoted their favorite verses each Sunday, one elderly man cited the same one every Sunday. His favorite verse was: "Grin and bear it." Many whine at life with a perpetual four-part anthem in a different minor key each day: "Nobody knows the trouble I've seen."

Can Christians respond to trials differently? James stressed that they can. Believers can face life's testing times with joy because they understand God's purposes in the test. People's outlook determines their outcome. However, believers must recognize the reality of life's testing times. James wrote, "when you meet various trials" (1:2), not: *if* you meet various trials. Testing times come to every believer. The Greek word translated "trials" may refer to testing or to tempting, depending on the context. In verse 13, the same word refers to temptation. In verse 2, it refers to tests which prove Christian character.

God tests believers to bring out the best; Satan tempts them to bring out the worst. A person chooses whether or not tests become temptations. Trials may refine people or ruin them, depending on their reactions. God's intention in every test of health or wealth is positive. The word **trial** indicates *a test that discovers the nature or quality of the person being tested.* James's words remind readers that whether they face trials is not the main point, but whether the trials make or break them. People may lose their wallets or their businesses. They may have blisters on their fingers or aneurysms on their arteries. They may have their plans for tomorrow crushed or their plans for a lifetime wrecked. The test may come in a doctor's diagnosis, a teenager's temper tantrum, friction at the office, or the pettiness of a good friend.

Although life's trials definitely come, they appear at indefinite times. The Greek word for "trials" gives the English word *pirate*. Like pirates, trials ambush the unsuspecting saint. James stressed that believers "fall" (KJV) into trials. That is a technicolor word. Jesus used the same word to indicate the hapless traveler to Jericho who suddenly "fell" into the midst of thieves (Luke 10:30). The same word indicated a ship that suddenly was stranded on a sand bar (Acts 27:41). James saw believers facing unwelcome, unexpected, and unavoidable encounters with life's tests.

More than coming at indefinite times, life's tests are personalized and synchronized. James used the colorful word translated "various" (1:2). The word could be translated *multicolored.* In the Septuagint, the same word was used to refer to Joseph's many-colored coat. A trial comes to match every color of one's personality. Trials have people's zip codes and thumbprints on them. What may shake the foundations of one person's life may not even touch another. God asked only Abraham, not Joseph or Moses, to sacrifice his son. Jesus asked only the rich young ruler to sell everything, not Nicodemus. He had a trial matched to test the faith of each person, but no trials were exactly alike.

Trials not only come personalized, but they also come synchronized, all at once. Shakespeare said: "When sorrows come, they come not single spies, But in battalions."[2] Everything happens at once. Trials of health lead to trials of wealth. These lead to vocational trials, domestic trials, and emotional trials. Jesus' closing parable in the Sermon on the Mount (Matt. 7:24-27) is about two builders who faced rain on the roof, wind on the walls, and water rising up to eat away the foundation—all at the same time. "Various trials" are just that: many simultaneous testing times.

Realize the Reaction of a Christian

The Christians' outlook determines their outcome in testing times. Rather than run, rejoice! My paraphrase of James 1:2 is: *Deem it an occasion of pure joy whenever you are ambushed by life's tests.* James did not indicate that trials are a joy, and he did not mean that the greatest joy in life is a trial. Excellent Christians do not frolic their way to funerals, go hilariously to hospitals, or zestfully watch their bank accounts go to zero. The text indicates that believers can make trials an occasion of joy if they understand the trials' purpose. Even Jesus "for the joy that was set before him endured the cross, despising the shame" (Heb. 12:2).

At the higher levels of Christian living, one may count one's trials "all joy." Here the word "all" has an intensifying effect: unmixed joy. Sweetness more than bitterness and light more than shadow can be people's portion during life's testing times. Joy reflects pleasure in one's progress toward Christian maturity through trials. One can encounter every trial and can write over it the words, "permitted by the Father." He has a purpose for trials in individuals' lives—to make believers mature through trials.

No one can deny the difficulty of facing life's tests. James called for a radical, prior decision. One might paraphrase 1:2: *Count (deem, reckon) your trials to be occasions of joy before they come.* To turn trials into triumphs or irritations into edifications is not natural. James's words have the sharp, urgent snap of a command to adopt an attitude now, while things are going well. Everyone needs an international date line which one crosses in reference to trials. Each person needs to cross a continental divide which gives one a different view of life's tests. People do this best before the trial comes, not in the midst of the trial. Have you ever deliberately and thoughtfully adopted an attitude toward those days which are sure to come?

Reaffirm the Reason for Trials

People's outlook does determine their outcome. Christians may deem trials as occasions of joy because they understand God's purpose in the trials, but believers cannot be what they might have been without life's testing times. As athletes say: "No pain, no gain." Airplanes take off by overcoming the resistance of gravity and wind. Yet, the wind that resists them lifts them higher. Trials function like that in Christians' lives.

Life's tests prove the genuineness of a believer's faith: "for you know that the testing of your faith produces steadfastness" (1:3). To paraphrase, *Trials prove what is genuine in your faith*. Here, the word **testing** means *the results of the trial, the tested residue that remains after the trying time*. A refined, genuine element of true character remains after tribulation blows away the chaff. Peter expressed the same hope: "so that the genuineness of your faith, more precious than gold which though perishable is tested by fire, may redound to praise and glory and honor at the revelation of Jesus Christ" (1 Pet. 1:7). Just as the craftsman heats gold ore in order to skim away the dross, so God permits testing times in the believer's life. When the dross floats to the top, He skims it away so that He sees His face reflected in people's lives. That was Job's victorious shout after he had endured many tests: "When he has tried me, I shall come forth as gold" (Job 23:10).

Untested faith would be suspect. A ship built in drydock is not proved seaworthy until it hits gale-force winds. A raw recruit with six weeks' boot camp is not really battle proved until he has faced enemy fire. So faith must be proved on the battlefield of life.

Life's testing times also prove the durability of a person's faith: "The testing of your faith produces steadfastness" (1:3). This sort of steadfastness reveals itself in triumphant fortitude, unswerving constancy, and unending tenacity. Trials show one's capacity to stand up and take adversity—over and over. The Christian gospel is one of a good finish, not just a good start. God required Abraham to wait twenty-five years before giving him the son of promise. Joseph showed constancy for thirteen years from pit to prison before he reached the palace. Moses waited eighty years to discover God's crowning purpose for his life. In each instance, faith, through trials, displayed active patience. Listening to sermons, reading this book, or even praying cannot substitute for the laboratory of life in this regard.

Life's testing times develop the mature ripeness of people's faith. No one can buy synthetic maturity. Recently, an entrepreneur invented synthetic ice cream extracted from soybeans. It really tastes like ice cream, yet not a drop of cream is in it. No such shortcut to Christian growth exists. James stated the organic process of Christian maturity: "And let steadfastness have its full effect, that you may be perfect and complete, lacking in nothing" (1:4). Christians must not short-circuit the chain of events described in 1:3-4. My paraphrase is: *Keep on letting steadfast endurance work its way out in your life.* Such unswerving tenacity will lead to mature ripeness in Christian character. This process ultimately will make one "perfect" (1:4).

The word "perfect" does not imply that one can become sinless or absolutely without flaw in this life. The word does indicate that life's trials help every grace reach its ripe maturity in one's life. Believers need not be stunted in any essential of the Christian life. Not only can they be mature but also "complete" (1:4). The word "complete" indicates anything with all its parts present; no part is missing or inadequate. Together, both words represent a well-rounded, full-grown Christian experience.

In order to make steel a thing of value, craftsmen must temper it. The process requires that the raw metal be heated glowing hot and then plunged into a solution of brine or oil. This produces a screaming hiss of metal and liquid. However, the steel that is produced has a hardness that comes in no other way. God tempers believers through testing times.

If believers understood testings better, they might sing: *Count your many trials, name them one by one, and it will surprise you what the Lord has done.* In this regard, Christians need to be like oysters. Whenever an irritation lodges in an oyster, the oyster turns a problem into a pearl. Every irritation can be edification and every trial a triumph. One's outlook determines the outcome.

Wisdom—The Resource for Testing Times (1:5-8)

Facing testing times with a mature outlook demands insight beyond oneself. One arrives at a necessary recognition: "if any of you lacks wisdom" (1:5). The qualifying "if" should not mislead anyone. The words should be understood to mean: *Since individuals among you are deficient in wisdom.* The text implies that some believers came short of the wisdom that was needed to turn trials into triumphs. James fixed on individual responsibility to recognize this fact.

To face life's quizzes with the right outlook requires continual intercession—perpetual requests to God. When a person needed wisdom, James wrote: "Let him ask God . . ." (1:5). The phrase does not imply permission as much as it does a mandate. The habitual duty of one who is deficient in wisdom must be to ask God continually for insight. James must have been recalling Jesus' repeated teaching. Jesus stressed persistence in prayer.

Surely, James and his readers understood verse 5 to be an allusion to Solomon's youthful request for wisdom (1 Kings 3:7). Solomon begged God for wisdom that would be equal to his task. God quickly gave him the requested wisdom for a specific, difficult problem or case (1 Kings 3:16-28). James assured all believers that each one had the same privilege before God as the famous king had.

God's Generous Goodness

God does not give with a closed fist; He gives with an open hand. He is a God who gives to all persons liberally (Jas. 1:5). Generously and simply, God gives the asking believer wisdom. His gift is without reservation, hesitation, or calculation for a return gift. The text implies that God gives a person wisdom without any secondary motive or deceit. He gives with a single-minded generosity.

James literally called God *the giving God*. The force of the expression is difficult to translate. God's giving is not so much an act as it is a habit. He must give as surely as the sun must give light as it burns or as a flower gives fragrance as it blooms. God's giving is part of His nature. When believers ask Him to give wisdom, they do not ask Him to do a strange thing.

When a person asks God for wisdom, God gives such wisdom positively: He gives "without reproaching" (1:5). God does not rebuke, criticize, or complain when one asks Him for wisdom. James specifically meant that God does not reproach the believer for what he/she did with God's last gift. He never says: *What did you do with the last gift I gave you? You have wasted everything else; why should I help you now?* No, God does not despise ordinary, blundering people who come again and again. That God gives is wonderful. That He gives liberally is more wonderful. One may go to Him a thousand times. One may go with needs as great as a vacant ocean. One even may go to Him after years of ingratitude. God does not reproach those who ask.

God's Giving—People's Receiving

James moved from the quality of divine giving to the quality of human receiving. Attention shifted from the willing Father to the waiting child. The seeker for wisdom in trials must pray in a single atmosphere. "Let him ask in faith" (1:6). The petitioner must approach habitually, with faith in God's character and in His ability to give. The best comment is Hebrews 11:6: "Without faith it is impossible to please him. For whoever would draw near to God must believe that he exists and that he rewards those who seek him." The Christian must come to God with a wholehearted confidence that He will heed one's request.

Even more emphatically, James urged believers to come "with no doubting" (1:6). The Greek word for doubting suggested a critical state of mind constantly hesitating and being indecisive. Such an attitude always debates with itself about God's character. It oscillates between belief and unbelief. What specific doubt did James have in mind? He seemed to indicate that an inner civil war exists between trust and distrust of God. This may be at the point of God's ability to grant one's request or at the point of His willingness to do so. Others have thought that James had in mind a practical doubting which wavers between God and the world. Such a prayer hesitates between friendship with the world and allegiance to God. (See 4:4.)

When believers pray with doubting and wavering, they demonstrate a radical defect in their approach to God. James vividly portrayed such a person as a "wave of the sea that is driven and tossed by the wind" (1:6). Divine wisdom cannot be given to a mind that is tossed here and there by doubt about God's character. James knew from the storms on the Sea of Galilee what a maverick wave could do to unsettle and frighten people. (See Luke 8:24.)

Christians who are blown about by doubt and disbelief in their prayer life face disaster. God insists only that one believe that He exists and that He has the kind of goodwill toward the one praying that a father has toward his children. Do you see a gathering storm of instability in your life? God wants you to pray and not to be like the wind-driven surge, but to be like the strong current of a rapid river that sweeps away obstacles as it bears steadily onward into the ocean of divine grace. As always, Jesus said it best: " 'Truly, I say to you, if you have faith and never doubt, you will not only do what has been done to the fig tree, but even if you say to this mountain, "Be taken up and cast into the sea," it will be done. And whatever you ask in prayer, you will receive, if you have faith' " (Matt. 21:21-22).

Double-Minded Saints

What is the result of the kind of "seasick" praying that James described in verse 6? James warned emphatically: "That person must not suppose that a double-minded man, unstable in all his ways, will receive anything from the Lord" (1:7-8). Such a wavering Christian might make an unwarranted judgment. He might imagine a divine answer to such divided praying. James set the record straight: Such praying receives neither wisdom for trials nor anything else. With the phrase "that person," James disassociated himself from the doubting individual with a hint of disapproval or contempt. Divided praying finds that heaven is a brass canopy.

Indeed, the divided person is "double-minded" (v. 7). Literally, the Greek word can be rendered *two-souled*. James coined a word that was used nowhere else in the Greek language before his time. Doubting, wavering praying literally houses a divided mind or heart. The Old Testament provided James with this concept. Every Jew repeated daily that God is one and should be loved with an undivided heart (Deut. 6:4-5). Doubleness of heart is the essence of sin in the Old Testament. (See Ps. 12:1-2.) The essence can be caught by visualizing someone who straddles the fence.

Further, the divided person who is drawn in two directions reveals instability in "all his ways" (Jas. 1:8). His heart reflects the instability of a kingdom where no one person rules. With the fickleness that characterizes a boy who loves one girl friend today and another tomorrow, so that person prays. As Moffatt translated: "He is . . . wavering at every turn."[3] What is worse, his praying affects his whole conduct in life in all that he does. Vacillating prayer leads one to an indecisive walk. Such a divided person displays instability throughout his life. One who cannot trust God may not be trustworthy.

Poor Man, Rich Man—Two Tests (1:9-11)

Two tests are common to life everywhere: the test of plenty and the test of want. James addressed the test of poverty and the test of affluence. Whereas some interpreters view this as an entirely new subject, it likely is a continuation of James's treatment of life's tests. He moved from the general discussion of trials (1:2-8) to specific tests that require a full use of divine wisdom.

The Test of Poverty

First, James wrote of the Christian brother in a difficult economic situation: "Let the lowly brother boast in his exaltation" (1:9). The person whom James identified was a Christian brother. Yet, the Christian brother found himself in "lowly" circumstances. The word "lowly" suggests one who was poor, oppressed, humble, and seemingly unimportant. The early church's records suggest that many of its members were from the lowest economic levels of society. The burial inscriptions in catacombs at Rome reveal a huge number of slaves who embraced Christianity. For many in James's day, Christ was their only hope.

What should such poor, oppressed people do? James encouraged them to boast in their high spiritual position. He did not mean that every poor person was blessed spiritually by poverty. He meant just the opposite, for poverty can embitter and ruin people. While physically poor, they are spiritually rich. They should "rejoice in . . . [their] exalted station" (Williams).[4] The joy of this kind of reversal of fortune animated Mary's great Magnificat or exalted song which she sang (Luke 1:46-55). Mary was the mother of Jesus and James. She exulted that in the incarnation, God "'has put down the mighty from their thrones, and exalted those of low degree'" (Luke 1:52). Perhaps this became a theme in Jesus and James's Nazareth home.

James urged that poor believers separate the present from the end time to come. The godless rich people arrogantly boasted in the present. The Christians enjoyed spiritual riches and would triumph in the world to come.

The Test of Affluence

James turned his attention to the rich man. Did James consider wealth a greater test of Christian character than poverty? Note that he wrote twice as much in warning the rich. Some scholars have doubted that the rich man (1:10) was even a Christian. They have seen James's warning as being like Jesus' warning about the rich fool (Luke 12:13-21). However, in parallel with 1:9, to understand that the rich man was a Christian brother is best. Although such cases were rare in the early church, they were not nonexistent.

An affluent believer was to boast in his spiritual humiliation. This sense of self-abasement should have come from his identification with Christ and His poor people. Furthermore, he was to recognize his own sin and the fleeting character of human wealth. Out of all this, he would be able to walk before God and people in humility, not in the arrogance of the proud rich. Before the affluent believer's eyes remained the reminder: "like the flower of the grass he [the proud rich person] will pass away" (1:10). Elsewhere, James wrote of the uncertain character of life (4:14).

A vivid illustration of the sudden reversal of fortunes for the worldly rich people is the burning east wind from the Syrian desert. At first light, the emerald grass and delicate wildflower kiss the morning dew. Yet by midday, the blast of the desert wind will leave only parched, blighted ground. The flower of the morning is fit only for fuel in the communal clay oven in the afternoon. No one ever has seen a hearse with a U-Haul trailer behind it. Much of

people's efforts to secure life financially is like rearranging the deck chairs on the Titanic. Or, as one familiar statement says, shrouds have no pockets.

A Beatitude for Testing Times (1:12)

James closed his section on testing times with a personal beatitude for the believer who faced life's tests. Whether the man was rich or poor, he was blessed if he faced the trial with steadfast endurance and triumphant fortitude. The word "blessed" suggested someone who shared in the life of God. Such a person enjoyed a divine sufficiency in life, regardless of circumstances. When such a person has stood the test, he will receive the victor's wreath. James employed a term that was used for those who had qualified for the athletic games. For the Christian, that wreath will be eternal life. Beyond the cross of trial is the crown of life.

Tempting Times (1:13-17)

One must distinguish carefully between testing times and tempting times. God permits tests so that believers might show the genuineness and durability of their faith. Temptation does not come from God. Testing times may become tempting times if the believer mishandles them. Yet, no one may blame God for temptations to sin (1:13).

As he liked to do, James placed a statement in the mouth of a detractor: "I am tempted by God" (1:13). This style of writing was called the diatribe style and probably reflected doubters or opponents as they interrupted early Christian preaching. James responded that God is not even the remote source of temptation. He cannot be tempted to do evil; He literally is untemptable. As asbestos is to fire, so God resists temptation—absolutely. He cannot be tempted even with the desire to tempt anyone! Perhaps James's opponent blamed God for human lust.

Late one night, I rode across a remote stretch of desert on the way back to an airport after a speaking engagement. On the long trip, a pastor shared his burden. A young woman in his church came for counsel. She shared that God had revealed to her that she must marry a certain man in the church. To the pastor's shock, that man was a married deacon. I counseled the pastor to confront the young lady with James 1:13. We must use God's Word to reveal such moral confusion for what it is. God does not relate even remotely to such errors.

Anatomy of a Temptation

James dramatically portrayed the process of temptation. Led by the Holy Spirit, he displayed the keenest perception of human nature. Ultimately, "each person" (1:14) is nailed with the responsibility for his/her own temptations. Ever since Adam blamed Eve, people have shown an innate tendency to shift the blame for sin to someone else. Today, people blame economic, social, educational, and even genetic factors for their failure to live responsibly under God. James riveted the blame directly where it belonged—on the sinner. He indicated that the culprit is lust ("desire," 1:14). Unfortunately, this word always has sexual overtones in today's world. Actually, the word referred to any strong desire outside of God's will. It might be desire for fame, position, power, wealth, or illicit sexual relations.

To describe the allure of lust, James used terms from the world of hunting and fishing. "Lured and enticed" (1:14) belonged to the sporting world. "Lured" indicated drawing a fish out of repose with bait. "Enticed" referred to drawing an animal to a trap with bait. The two terms graphically presented lust's unsettling deception. James pictured a believer at rest in the settled restraint of disciplined living. Suddenly the bait was presented, and the person was lured out of rest. When he took the bait, he was surprised that he had been caught and could not escape.

In 1:15, James changed the figure of speech from the sporting world to that of an illegitimate birth. Lust is personified as an evil seductress who entices a person and then conceives a terrible offspring. When lust gives birth, the birth certificate records the name: sin. When sin reaches maturity, it, too, takes part in a terrible conception. Sin produces the monstrous offspring, death. James traced three generations of an awful family: lust, sin, and death. Only God's liberating act in Christ can stop this terrible genealogy and transfer a person to God's family.

The Father of Lights

To attribute the dark process of lust, sin, and death to God is an error that strikes at the heart of faith. James charged believers to stop being deceived at this point (1:16). God is never the Father in this terrible family of darkness. He always is the "Father of lights"

(1:17), for He created all heavenly luminaries. The Milky Way galaxy in which planet earth orbits contains a million suns brighter than earth's sun. If one could travel at the speed of light (186,000 miles per second), it would take about 100,000 years just to cross the Milky Way. Yet this is just one galaxy among millions. God created all the lights in all the galaxies.

Furthermore, God created all moral and spiritual lights. Christ embodied this light. John wrote that in Christ, "the true light that enlightens every man was coming into the world" (John 1:9). James indicated that God is light that never can be eclipsed: "There is no variation" with Him (1:17). James's phrase "no . . . shadow due to change" could refer to an astronomical eclipse or to the change of seasons. On earth, the amount and intensity of light varies with the change of seasons. With God, no such variation occurs. He is such light that not even a shadow can be cast on Him. While one may worry about changes in the stock market, the international situation, or personal health, one need not worry about God's nature. Yesterday, today, and tomorrow, He is the source of totally good gifts.

Born by the Word (1:18)

God does not give birth to temptation but to regeneration. Lust gives birth to sin and death. God's Word gives the new birth. In 1:18, birth by the Word is a deliberate contrast to the awful birth of sin in 1:15. The instrument by which spiritual birth comes is God's Word. This fastens an awesome responsibility on those who proclaim and teach that Word. James saw the first generation of believers as the "first fruits of his creatures" (1:18). In the Old Testament, the Israelites offered the first part of their crops as an acknowledgement that the whole harvest belonged to God. More was to come, and it would be the result of God's blessings. Even so, James saw in the scattered communities of Jewish Christians the first fruits of a great harvest which was to come.

Lessons for Life from James 1:1-18

Every believer should prepare in advance for life's testing times. Have your family members discussed how they would respond in the face of life's tests of health and wealth? One godly young couple lost their little son in a tragic accident. Part of their response was to bring their offering by the Sunday School department as they were on their way to the funeral home to make final selections. Such disciplined living does not come without prior commitment.

Increasingly, affluent Christians must come to grips with their wealth. Baptists are becoming an incredibly wealthy people. Along with this comes the temptation to covet, to grasp, and to hold more and more. However, one should develop the discipline to hold life's material things with an easy grip.

Avoid the temptation to blame God for moral and spiritual failures. Many people complain to God: "Why did you make me this way?" This does not excuse irresponsible rebellion against God. People must assume responsibility for their choices and acts. They must acknowledge what they are before they, in repentance, can disown what they are.

Recognize that everything deserving the name good comes from God. Insurance companies refer to natural tragedies as "acts of God." This may reflect the human tendency to blame God for bad things rather than to praise Him for good things. Have you paused to take inventory of life's blessings? God always deserves praise, never blame.

------

1. C. Leslie Mitton, *The Epistle of James* (Grand Rapids, Mich.: William B. Eerdmans Publishing Co., 1966), p. 16.

2. *Hamlet*, act 4, sc. 5., lines 75-78.

3. From *The Bible: a New Translation* by James A. R. Moffatt. Copyright © 1935 by Harper and Row, Publishers, Inc. Used by permission.

4. From *The New Testament, a Translation in the Language of the People*, by Charles B. Williams. Copyright 1937 and 1966. Moody Press, Moody Bible Institute of Chicago. Used by permission.

Personal Learning Activities

1. According to Dr. Gregory, the author of the Letter of James was (choose the correct answer from the list):
   ___(1) James the son of Al-   ___(3) James, Jesus' half
   phaeus.   brother.

___(2) James the son of Zebedee.   ___(4) An unknown James.

2. According to James, life's trials _____ _____. (Choose the proper response from the list.)
   (1) Are a means of judgment
   (2) Are signs of God's displeasure
   (3) Are to be endured grudgingly
   (4) Prove what is genuine in one's faith

3. James wrote that one must ask God for wisdom (select the correct answer from the list):
   ___(1) In faith, without doubting.
   ___(2) As a last resort.
   ___(3) Repeatedly.
   ___(4) Boldly.

4. According to Dr. Gregory, two tests common to life everywhere are _____ and _____. (Choose the proper responses from the list.)
   (1) Sickness
   (2) Plenty
   (3) Pain
   (4) Want
   (4) Stress
   (6) Aging

5. James stated that temptations ultimately come from God.
   ___True ___False

Answers:

1. (3); 2. (4); 3. (1); 4. (2),(4); 5. False.

2
Doing
the Word
James 1:19-27

"Now hear this!" These words ring familiar to many veterans of military service. Just such a command opens James 1:19-27: "Know this, my beloved brethren" (1:19). James softened what he wrote with a reminder of his relationship to the readers. They were "beloved brethren." Born of the same Father, they shared a fraternal love. Nevertheless, James used an imperative, a command. He had reminded his readers of the life-giving character of the "word of truth" (1:18). Evidently, he feared that some of his readers could not hear that Word. Nothing physical deafened them. James sensed that they could not hear because they had too much to say themselves, and some of them were angry about it!

Hearing the Word (1:19-21)

Today's Christian has access to countless words from God. Radio, television, tapes, conferences, seminars, films, and books—not to mention church services—all present God's Word. How should one listen? James counseled the believer to listen quickly: "Be quick to hear" (1:19). This demand did not refer to general daily conversation. In the context, it referred directly to hearing

God's Word. "Quick" translates a word from which the English word *tachometer* comes. This instrument measures how fast any piece of machinery operates. The believer should respond to opportunities for hearing the Word swiftly, not reluctantly.

Closely related to the demand to be "quick to hear" is the exhortation that the believer listen to the Word of God quietly: "Be . . . slow to speak." Richard Foster observed: "If we hope to move beyond the superficialities of our culture . . . we must be willing to go down into the recreating silences."[1] Perhaps James's readers experienced noisy church services such as those in Corinth. In such services, everyone wanted to talk, and no one wanted to listen (1 Cor. 14:26-33). Long before James, another wise writer warned: "Do you see a man who is hasty in his words? There is more hope for a fool than for him" (Prov. 29:20). G. B. Duncan observed: "God still comes where he can find someone quiet enough to listen and alone enough to heed."[2]

James urged his readers to listen to God's Word calmly: "Be . . . slow to anger" (Jas. 1:19). The phrase suggests the danger of smoldering resentment or wrath. When such anger burns in a person's heart, the Word of God cannot share the same quarters. When believers harbor inner rage, God's Word cannot be heard.

People's anger never accomplishes God's righteous purpose: "The anger of man does not work the righteousness of God" (1:20). Not only does rage keep one from hearing God's Word, but it also fails to produce God's purposes in the world. Smoldering, resentful wrath is wrong. James may have had in mind outbursts among Christians or resentment against persecutors. Bitter anger falls short of God's standard in one's life and fails to work out God's righteous program in the world. Such anger may work powerfully in the secular political world, but it is utterly alien to God's kingdom. Perhaps James remembered Jesus' awesome, stern words concerning anger. (See Matt. 5:21-22.) In Jesus' new order, destructive anger deserves the same punishment as murder in the old order.

God wanted Moses to lead the Exodus. Yet, Moses first tried the right thing the wrong way. From anger, he murdered an Egyptian for beating a Hebrew (Ex. 2:12). He tried to perform God's will through human anger. Moses learned the painful lesson that God will do His work in His way.

Can you remember any occasion when anger furthered God's cause between two believers? Has an outburst in a church business meeting ever forwarded Christ's cause? Such a case would be

24

rare if not nonexistent. According to Will Rogers, "People who fly into a rage always make a bad landing."[3].

Dealing with anger alone is not enough. James called for decisive disposal of every attitude that hinders the inward work of the Word: "Therefore put away all filthiness and rank growth of wickedness" (1:21). A person who is careful about his/her appearance quickly removes a soiled garment. James's word refers to a resolute removal of a stained garment. Some attitudes soil the covering of Christian character. James suggested: *Change clothes immediately.* The Christian should remove everything of any kind that suggests moral uncleanness and greed. James's word denoted various kinds of filth, and it even was used for disgusting earwax. Such filth plugs up the spiritual ear so that God's Word cannot enter. Likewise, the believer must strip off "rank . . . wickedness" or ill will, the desire to injure another. The thought implies the dangerous capacity of malicious wickedness to overflow the banks of control.

A Christian must not adopt a policy of gradual elimination for the moral monsters that James pointed out. One must strike a death blow immediately. God's Word mandates that the believer drive a silver nail through the dark heart of all filthy wickedness. The human body does just this physically. With the help of a microscope, Lennart Nilsson captured on film the process by which the body seeks and destroys all impurities. White blood cells ooze around the impurities and engulf them. At this point, the process looks like a misshapen, undefined blob. Then, an eerie glow appears as the cells first absorb and then literally explode the impurity. The body deals decisively with invading impurity. James called on the spiritual life to deal just as drastically with all moral impurities.[4]

Implanting the Word (1:21)

When believers decisively eradicate sin, they are preparing for a spiritual implant: "Receive with meekness the implanted word, which is able to save your souls" (1:21). In contrast to anger which blocks God's Word, one must welcome His Word with an attitude of meekness. Often, meekness is misunderstood. It indicates an attitude of gentle considerateness; it is a receptivity that is the opposite of angry self-assertion. One hot September evening, a new student rang the doorbell to the president's office at Union Theological Seminary. "A man in shirt sleeves answered the door and led the student to the dormitory office. 'Are you the janitor?' asked the student. 'No, but I try to be helpful to the janitor.' "[5] The speaker, who did not identify himself, was the president of the seminary. Such gentle consideration speaks of fertile soil for the Word of God.

Today, we hope to prolong life with organ implants. James cautioned his readers to allow God to save spiritual life with a spiritual implant: His Word. In verse 21, James used an expression that appears nowhere else in the New Testament. He wrote of God's Word as "implanted" within the believer. The background of this idea may have been Jesus' parable of the sower (Matt. 13:1-9). Preaching sows the life-giving seed in human hearts. James warned that believers must take care to give the seed a fertile reception.

Readers may be familiar with the process by which implants that are grafted into native root stock produce beautiful hybrid roses. Tyler, Texas, enjoys fame as the rose capital of the world. The native Tyler rosebush has the finest root system; but it has only a poor, stunted bloom. When workers implant buds from beautiful hybrids into the native root stock, an extraordinary and beautiful rosebush grows. God designed human nature with the capacity to welcome His implanted Word. Such an implant ultimately leads to the rescue of the whole person at the last day.

Practicing the Word (1:22-25)

The implant alone is not enough. The Word that is planted within a person calls for the Word to be practiced without: "But be doers of the word, and not hearers only, deceiving yourselves" (1:22). The authentic believer continually strives for more and more practical obedience to the Word that already has been implanted. The "word" indicates particularly Jesus' ethical teachings. Jesus ended His great Sermon on the Mount with this emphasis. Hearing and doing build life on an unshakable rock. Hearing without doing undermines life and results in disaster at the end (Matt. 7:21-27). In biblical culture, the word "hearers" identified those who attended a lecture without becoming disciples. James favored the "doers." Doer was a word that he used four of its six times in the New Testament. People who hold that hearing alone is enough deceive themselves at the point of their own salvation. Such deception betrays ultimate spiritual danger. An anonymous believer noted: "Christ's sheep are marked in the ear and the foot; they hear his voice and they follow him."[6] Doers of the Word are the only hearers who respond in the right manner. James continued with an unforgettable illustration of the difference between hearing and doing.

First, James gave the negative example (1:23-24); then, he gave the positive example (1:25). A rushed person's casual glance into a poor mirror illustrates those who hear God's Word without being obedient. The context suggests a man who only glances at his face.

The mirror of biblical times usually consisted of bronze, copper, tin, and sometimes silver polished to reflect light. Such a mirror certainly gave an inferior reflection. The man peeked at his temporal, mortal face. True to life, he glanced at his face and forgot what he saw. Suddenly and permanently, he turned away from the mirror. The process left no lasting effect. When the mirror was left behind, the impression was gone. How many church members deal with God's Word in that fashion? How many can remember the text of last Sunday's sermon?

To read God's Word and see someone else's picture in it is easy. To gaze into that Word and see oneself is another matter.

Positively, the believer who hears and practices God's Word is like a man who carefully looks into a perfect mirror (1:25). James dropped the figure of a mirror and pictured the believer bending over the perfect law (God's ripe fulfillment of the Law in Jesus and His teachings). Unlike a poor metal mirror, Jesus' Word in the Gospels is perfect. Jesus claimed that His reinterpretation of Moses' law fulfilled that law (Matt. 5:17). Jesus made the Law perfect in two senses: (1) He perfectly embodied and kept the Law. In His teachings, the Law rose to its perfect intention. (2) What is more, Jesus' perfect law gives liberty. To most people, the word "law" indicates confinement and restriction. Yet Jesus' law liberates those who obey it. They experience a new freedom that previously they had not known. What is more, the blessing in keeping Jesus' law does not come after obedience; it comes in the midst of obeying the law. Obedient keepers of Jesus' law of liberty receive their own personal beatitude.

The laws that God has woven into His universe give liberty. Music does not result from random banging on a piano keyboard. Musicians must confine themselves to the discipline of the lines, spaces, key signatures, and so forth, that make music what it is. Artists must confine themselves to a canvas, golfers to an inside or outside swing, and motorists to the rules of the road. In each instance, not to find the laws involved will lead to chaos and failure. The Ten Commandments set Israel free from the chaos of anarchy. In a much greater way, Christ's new law set one absolutely free, not only in outward act but in inward attitude. Lawless living is slavery. Perfect law produces perfect liberty. If you think not, consider the chaos and paralysis that would tyrannize each home and family if God gave no law for the husband, the wife, and the children. Are households that are ignorant of God's law really free? Are they not slaves to the chaos of unregulated life? Are they not like ships that navigate treacherous waters without a compass? God's law sets people free.

Human language fails when it attempts to describe the Word of God. James called that Word a seed which God implants (1:21). Just as a seed does, the Word contains the power to germinate, root itself, and grow. From another perspective, God's Word is a mirror. Unlike any natural mirror, it shows people what they are in sin; and it also shows what they can be in righteousness. Finally, God's Word is a perfect law. Every human statute falls short of perfection and cannot make anyone perfect. God's law is perfect and ultimately will make perfect those who keep it in Christ.

Do you spend as much time preparing the soil of your heart for the Word as you do preparing the soil of your lawn or garden? Do you spend as much time gazing into the mirror of the Word as you do the mirror on the wall? Do you dare not forget the city's laws but forget the Lord's law?

Real Religion (1:26-27)

James never was content with the general; he was particular about doing the Word. Real religion includes taming the tongue, helping the helpless, and maintaining personal purity from the world.

If persons claim real religion, they must tame the tongue. James mentioned an aspect of speech in every chapter of his letter. James 3:1-12 well may be the greatest passage on the tongue in the Bible. James suggested that the tongue is a wild beast that must be tamed (3:7-8). In 1:26, he focused on one who seemed to be religious but did not control his speech. Such a person fancied that he was genuinely pious. That person's emphasis rested on the externals of religious performance. He was addicted to forms of religion. For the Jewish Christians to whom James wrote, religious externals included prayer, fasting, worship, and almsgiving. Remember that Jesus sternly warned against the danger of religious form without content (Matt. 6:1-18). Yet for all of his religious activity, the man who only followed religious forms failed to "bridle" his tongue. This is the first biblical use of the word "bridle" to refer to the tongue. Such a vivid word aptly describes the untamed potency of the unwatched tongue.

External religious activity minus disciplined speech uncovers a person's self-deception. Here, the danger is not hypocrisy; it is self-deception. Such a person feels religiously authentic, but in reality he possesses only counterfeit Christianity. Deception seizes his heart—the center of personal life. What is more, all of his external religious activity is uselessly empty. Like a nutshell without a kernel inside, his religious activity reveals a disappointing inner emptiness. James's word for "vain" pointed particularly to the worship of idols in the Old Testament. He believed that such undisciplined religion without controlled conversation might be as unprofitable as bowing before an idol.

A woman came during the invitation. She was earnest in her search for God. After the pastor asked her several questions, he found her to be distressed by her Christian employer's harshness. He suggested that she find other employment. When the girl lifted her head, the pastor discovered that she was his housekeeper. Conviction gripped him because he had nullified his witness with his unbridled tongue.[7]

Who cannot identify with that story? How many chant, "O, for a thousand tongues to sing" on Sunday; yet they use their tongues to contradict their witness on Monday? Why not take an inventory of those situations where undisciplined speech may overcome a person? Husband-wife discussions about money, schedules, or child rearing often set the scene for heated words. Office gossip sessions about an absent co-worker can contradict Christian profession. Relaxed recreational settings sometimes loosen the tongues of otherwise disciplined disciples.

Real religion is a contrast to empty ceremony (1:27). Help for the helpless and personal purity mark real faith. James did not mean that religion exhausts God's will. However, he did view real religion as exemplary of genuine Christianity. Authentic Christianity is described positively as "pure" and negatively as "undefiled," without filth. Together, these two terms signify absolute purity. Unfortunately, as the Old Testament period had progressed, such words had drifted toward mere correctness of religious ceremony. James took up the prophetic demand that God does not desire pure ceremony as much as He desires pure people.

Additionally, real religion is pure "before God." For religious performance to impress people is one thing. Some people can give academy award performances of religious activities. But for God to view their acts as pure is another thing. What kind of activity pleases the discerning eye of the Almighty? One pleases God when that person cares for people who are helpless. In the Old

Testament, "orphans and widows" represented all those who were without defense, protection, or provision. Remember that no so-cial-security or child-welfare organizations existed. The loss of a husband or parents often meant total disaster. Widows sometimes became prostitutes, and orphans were sold into slavery. James wrote that as a habit of life, sincere Christians should look in on ("visit") such need. The text calls for more than a single instance and more than secondhand charity. James meant more than merely to call on those who were in need; the term translated **visit** meant *to assume responsibility for and to support.*

In a closely related demand, James called for personal purity. Genuine believers guard against contact with pervading moral pollution in the culture around them. In James's sense, "the world" indicates the spirit of the age—in every age—which reflects a godless agenda for personal and community life. While witnessing Christians are to love the lost world of humanity, they should shun the spirit of the age. Believers are to correct the spirit of the age, not catch it.

Real religion must incarnate itself into life, not just generally but particularly, in actual cases. W. A. Criswell related the following disturbing poem:

"A certain pastor of great austerity
Climbed up in his high church steeple
To be nearer God that he might hand
God's word down to the people.
He cried from his steeple,
"Where art Thou, Lord?"
And the Lord replied,
"I'm down here with my people."
—Anonymous[8]

God's concern for starving children, lonely widows in a rest home, and the empty-eyed transients on the street is as real as His concern for busy church programs.

Lessons for Life from James 1:19-27

Listen to God's Word quietly and calmly.—One should have a definite preparation when approaching the Word of God. A great golfer such as Jack Nicklaus has consistent approaches for the various shots that he must make. How much more discipline should the believer bring to preparation for hearing God's Word? In private devotional life, one should find a place of quietness and stillness. Sit with your eyes closed in meditation until the hurry and anger of the day fades. Sometimes, deep and controlled breathing for several minutes helps the believer to concentrate on the Word.

Deal with anger before it deals with you.—The mental, spiritual, and physical impact of anger destroys life. One needs to make a decisive, life-changing decision concerning anger. With great deliberation, decide once-and-for-all that anger does not pay. This one great decision will help with a thousand little decisions to rid yourself of rage.

Dare to make a list of religious professions versus religious practices.—On one side of the page, write what you profess to believe. Opposite that, write the concrete impact in life. Do you believe that God is merciful? When did you last show mercy? Do you believe that God loves you and others unconditionally and forgives freely? When did you last forgive someone without attaching any strings?

Inventory your personal religious activities.—Which activities are merely external with no inner spiritual significance? Which activities actually show God's concern for the helpless people? What should be added and subtracted from your weekly round of "religious" activities to align yourself with God's priorities?

1. John Blanchard, *Gathered Gold* (Bath, England: The Pitman Press, 1984), p. 200.

2. Ibid., p. 288.

3. Ibid., p. 5.

4. See Paul Brand and Philip Yancy, *Fearfully and Wonderfully Made* (Grand Rapids, Mich.: Zondervan, 1980), pp. 17-18.

5. Clyde E. Fant, Jr. and William M. Pinson, Jr., *20 Centuries of Great Preaching* (Waco, Tex.: Word Books, Pub., 1971), 8:281.

6. Blanchard, p. 208.

7. Spiro Zodhiates, *The Work of Faith* (Chattanooga, Tn.: AMG Publishers, n.d.), pp. 133-34.

8. Cited by W. A. Criswell, *Expository Sermons on the Epistle of James* (Grand Rapids, Mich.: Zondervan Pub. House, 1975), p. 37.

Personal Learning Activities

1. In 1:19, James advised his readers to be quick to _____, slow to _____, and slow to _____.
2. James indicated that to hear the Word was sufficient for Chris-

tian living. ____True ____False

3. James defined the perfect law as (choose the correct answer from the list):
____(1) Restrictive.   ____(3) Difficult.
____(2) Harsh.   ____(4) The law of liberty.

4. James stated that one who really is religious must _____. (Select the proper response from the list.)
(1) Go to church   (3) Keep the law
(2) Tithe   (4) Bridle the tongue

5. According to James, what constitutes pure and undefiled religion?

Answers:

1. Hear, speak, anger; 2. False; 3. (4); 4. (4); 5. To visit orphans and widows, and to keep oneself unstained from the world.

33

3
Warning Against Partiality
James 2:1-13

" 'Full many people go to church,
As everyone knows;
Some go to close their eyes,
And some to eye their clothes.' "[1]

The little rhyme suggests the reason that James felt compelled to write 2:1-13. Even in the earliest Christian communities social, financial, and racial distinctions already caused tension. God intended that the church be the one place where every believer could meet on level ground.

Everybody Is Somebody (2:1-5)

Many church bulletins proclaim that everybody is somebody. Is that always the case? James sharply criticized a discriminating process that already was underway in the early church. He wrote: "Show no partiality as you hold the faith of our Lord Jesus Christ, the Lord of glory" (2:1). Actually, James condemned an attitude that already was evident. My paraphrase would be: *In practicing your faith, do not play favorites in the church.* James softened his appeal by calling his readers "my brethren." Beyond establishing a warm, fraternal relationship between the writer and readers, in the Letter of James this phrase indicates the beginning of a new section wherever it appears.

In verse 1, the word "faith" may indicate either the body of Christian belief or the warm, personal trust in Christ that alone secures personal salvation. James probably meant the latter. A person cannot play favorites in the church on the one hand and, on the other, claim to have an authentic, personal faith in Jesus Christ.

Partiality is one of the truly technicolor words in the Book of James. The word literally means *that which receives face* or *that which lifts up the face.* Either meaning fits well. The word may mean *to receive the face of another person in an evaluating way.* Such an attitude scans the features of a new face coming into the church. An instant evaluation takes place. Immediately, the evaluator categorizes the newcomer socially, educationally, and economically. On the basis of such a decision, fellowship is given or withdrawn. Or, James may have had another idea in mind. Many people cannot conceal their reaction to a newcomer. Their emotions write themselves on their faces. The text may refer to the accepting smile or the rejecting frown on the faces of church members when they reacted to new members. In either case, James condemned such superficial distinctions in the Christian fellowship.

Even the church's enemies and their spies recognized that Jesus did not show any partiality. Luke 20:21-22 records a question that Jesus' opponents asked Him. Even they recognized that Jesus did not show partiality. According to my literal translation, they said: *Teacher, we know that you . . . do not receive the face.* Nicodemus, the theologian, did not impress Jesus any more than the immoral woman at the well in Samaria. Jesus expressed the same interest in anonymous peasant children as He did toward adults who were impressed with their importance.

Repeatedly, the New Testament stresses that God will show no partiality in judging husbands, wives, children, slaves, and masters (Col. 3:25; Eph. 6:9). At the final judgment, every rank and category of people will stand on level ground. Paul insisted that God showed no partiality racially or religiously toward Jews or Greeks (Rom. 2:11). After Peter's liberating vision at Joppa, he confessed concerning the Roman centurion Cornelius: "'Truly I perceive that God shows no partiality'" (Acts 10:34). The entire Bible teaches God's absolute impartiality.

Have a Seat, Please (2:2-3)

James pictured two men coming to church. They may have been visitors or new converts. Both came to the Christian assembly (*synagogue* in Greek) seeking a seat. James recorded vividly how each appeared and where each was seated.

One man appeared with gold rings and fine clothes. Literally, the text reads: *having gold rings on his fingers in a bright toga.* Such a visitor veritably dripped gold from his fingers; he was a gold-fingered man. In ancient cultures, such rings sometimes could be rented in order that a person might give the impression of affluence. In ancient Greek culture, to wear such a ring was the equivalent of having a hillside mansion in the most elite section of a city. The man whom James described might have been voted "Best-Dressed Man" of the city. He wore an elegant, luxurious, shining garment. One commentator has noted that such a white toga, or outer garment, was worn by Romans who were seeking political office. This person was impressive, and he would be seated in the best seat in the house. My translation is: *You, yourself, sit there beautifully (becomingly, honorably).* He was one of the so-called beautiful people and was seated in "a good place" (v. 3, KJV).

In sharp contrast to the impressive person, "a poor man in shabby clothing" (1:2) entered. The text does not imply that both men entered at the same moment. The story certainly would be more dramatic if they did. The "poor man" represented someone at the subsistence level of living. The word translated "poor man" suggests a cringing begger, someone who did not have enough food or clothes to get by. Today, one would think of a street person or a "bag lady." The poor person wore dirty, vile, shabby clothes in contrast to the affluent visitor's bright toga. He received a strikingly different reaction than the impressive visitor received. The presider demanded: "'Stand there,' or, 'Sit at my feet'" (2:3). The first alternative implies standing room only in some inconspicuous place. The second alternative refers to a debasing, humiliating place. The biblical world often used the footstool.

In the command, "sit at my feet," the speaker deliberately may have alluded to the Old Testament practice of placing one's enemies beneath his footstool. Who can forget the psalmist's reference to the footstool: "The Lord says to my lord: 'Sit at my right hand, till I make your enemies your footstool'" (110:1)? The footstool implied the place of humiliation and subordination. However, the man in question in James was not told to sit on the footstool; he was told to sit under the footstool (KJV). Since that was impossible, the text implies sitting on the floor by the speaker's footstool. A greater put-down hardly could be imagined.

An early church manual showed the seriousness with which the first Christian communities took James's word. That manual demanded that the leader take the place of humility rather than tell the poor visitor to take it:

> And if a poor man or woman either of the district or of the (other) districts should come in and there is no place for them, thou, presbyter, make place for such with all thy heart, even if thou wilt sit on the ground, that there should not be respecting the person of man but of God.[2]

Has the kingdom of God lost opportunity for world impact because discriminations between rich and poor take place? The Tennessee Williams family moved to another city during the famous playwright's childhood. His younger sister and he wanted to join a church's choir. Because of their situation, they "'were made to feel like social untouchables.'"[3] What if his talents for drama had been captured by the church rather than by the world? Will eternity reveal that one experience of rejection turned him away from the church?

The Judges Judged (2:4)

James rendered a verdict on the injudicious judges (v. 4). They had wavered by discriminating among believers and by displaying evil motives. James posed two questions, both of which demanded a Yes answer. Paraphrased, the questions would read: *You have made prejudiced distinctions among yourselves, have you not? You have become judges with evil thoughts, have you not?* James nailed them with the implications of their partiality. They could only answer, *Yes.*

Behind the word "distinctions" (2:4) may rest two ideas. The word may indicate wavering or doubting. In that sense, the readers had wavered or doubted the heart of the Christian faith. By their attitude of favoritism, they had denied the core of Christianity. They had become double-minded or divided, the trait that James had exposed in 1:6-8. Their favoritism revealed them to be divided people with a fragmented faith. Or, the word translated "distinctions" may mean *to separate or divide.* By judging and seating the two visitors as they did, the people betrayed a prejudiced division

37

among its members.

Behind the members' act in seating the two visitors lay their motive. The church members acted as judges who were motivated by evil thoughts. As opposed to God who *never* receives people according to their faces, the church members received people *only* according to their faces. Such activity was rooted in the evil one, not in God. As Jewish Christians, James's readers were familiar with the Old Testament demand: "'You shall do no injustice in judgment; you shall not be partial to the poor or defer to the great, but in righteousness shall you judge your neighbor'" (Lev. 19:15). These believers' conduct contradicted the basic teachings of the Old Testament, not to mention the New Testament faith.

Sociologist Gerhard Lenski made a study of Christian attitudes in the Detroit area. Basically, he found that Protestant churches desired people "'like us'" in socio-economic level.[4] Another investigator recorded specific examples of discrimination within the churches. One church opposed wearing choir robes for a children's Easter program. The purpose was to allow the children to display their new Easter outfits. The result was that several children who could not afford new clothes were absent. A further outcome of the event was that the poorer families showed no more interest in the church or in the Lord. A woman with a questionable background professed faith in Christ. For several weeks, she and her children came to the church. Then suddenly their attendance stopped. She complained that the church people made her feel she was beneath them. One leading member had warned people not to associate with her because of her past life. When she stopped coming, the regular members took an I-told-you-so attitude. They excused their prejudiced conduct by judging that she quit coming because her profession of faith was not real anyway.

If one doubts the relevance of James's warning, consider the following example. Suppose two families move to the community. Through unavoidable circumstances, one family is on welfare. The other family is industrious, respectable, and solidly middle-class. Who will receive the warmer welcome from the church visitors? Will the youth of both families be as eagerly invited to the youth trips? If the men of both families had equal spiritual qualifications, which one would be placed on the deacon body? One quickly might say that the poor family should be the object of the church's charity. Yet, so often, such people do not want charity nearly so much as they want dignity. They want to be included in the church and its activities.

God's Poor People (2:5)

The large number of poor people in the church in James's day betrayed no accident of fate. Deliberately, God had chosen the people who were poor in the material realm to be rich in the spiritual realm. With a sharp call to attention, James demanded his readers' focused interest. My paraphrase reads: *God has chosen the poor of this world to be rich in faith, has He not?* Once again, James used a leading question which demanded a Yes answer. The number of poor people in the church related to God's electing purposes. Literally, God chose the poor for Himself. God's election of individuals and groups is one of the Bible's unfathomable mysteries. The doctrine of election means that God saves people because He intends to do so. God chooses to save all persons; those who respond to Him in faith become part of His elect. A vital part of God's elective intention is the salvation of the poor. This does not mean that poverty merits salvation and wealth does not. It does not mean that no rich person can be saved and that all poor people are chosen for salvation.

Nevertheless, one cannot deny God's interest in the poor by His own sovereign choice. Jesus declared: "'Blessed are you poor, for yours is the kingdom of God'" (Luke 6:20). Even though the Gospel of Matthew has "'poor in spirit'" (Matt. 5:3), in Luke Jesus probably addressed the materially poor. Jesus' first sermon in His hometown synagogue began with the affirmation: "'The Spirit of the Lord is upon me, because he has anointed me to preach good news to the poor'" (Luke 4:18). Jesus identified the Spirit's activity in His ministry with God's concern for the poor. James scarcely could have missed hearing Jesus' sermon. When John the Baptist was imprisoned, he wanted to test the authenticity of Jesus' ministry. Jesus sent him this evidence: "The poor have good news preached to them" (Luke 7:22).

Without question, the early church consisted largely of poor people. Paul reminded the Corinthian Christians that God had not chosen them according to the world's social or economic priorities (1 Cor. 1:26-31). Poverty particularly marked the Palestinian Christian communities that were familiar to James. As early as Acts 11:29, one reads: "The disciples determined, every one according to his ability, to send relief to the brethren who lived in Judea." James, Peter, and John urged Paul to remember the poor Palestinian Jewish Christians (Gal. 2:10). Dark days befell the Palestinian poor people when James wrote his letter. Crises ravaged the peasantry, and depressed wages crushed the laborers. Also, famine ravaged

Palestine about AD 46-48. From the first, Jesus had a small number of affluent adherents. Nicodemus, Joseph of Arimathea, Joanna, and others ministered to the Lord from their substance (Luke 8:2). However, the central appeal of the gospel was to the poor people of the land. Hannah's haunting cry echoes throughout the Bible:

> He raises up the poor from the dust;
> he lifts the needy from the ash heap,
> to make them sit with princes
> and inherit a seat of honor (1 Sam. 2:8).

James promised to everyone who hoped as Hannah did that God deliberately chose the poor as "heirs of the kingdom which he has promised to those who love him" (2:5). The kingdom of God signifies God's reign which Jesus inaugurated in His first coming. Jesus will consummate God's reign in His second coming when He returns to rule in millennial righteousness. In Luke 6:20, Jesus' first Beatitude seemed to promise the poor people that both now in the inaugurated kingdom and then in the consummated kingdom the poor have a central place. The rich people have an inheritance now. It always is subject to perishing, defiling, and fading influences. In Jesus, the poor have an inheritance which is to come. It is "imperishable, undefiled, and unfading" (1 Pet. 1:4).

W. A. Criswell related a life-changing encounter with the poor that encouraged his downtown church to continue reaching out to all people. Not long after he became pastor of First Baptist Church, Dallas, he went to the church early one morning. He noticed a group gathered around one of the doorways of the sanctuary. Curious, he worked his way through the crowd. He saw a man on the steps with his hands stretched out toward the church door. The man was dead. He died reaching out to the church in the heart of the city. This caused W. A. Criswell to design a whole spectrum of "Good Shepherd" ministries to reach the neediest and poorest people in the community.

How many other churches have responded to the reach of the poor? Will Campbell observed: Americans are learning to forgive "'black people for being black. What they can't forgive is their being poor.'"[5] Campbell stated that overt bigotry has diminished and that the anger, fear, and hatred that once was directed at blacks has been redirected toward the poor persons who live in the midst of the American dream. They have become an embarrassment rather than an opportunity for ministry. He further stated that for the most part, churches do little to identify with the poor people as Christ did. They gear their programs to reach the middle class and largely ignore the poor. One must ask: What does my church do directly for the poor? James considered concern for the help-less poor persons to be the earmark of authentic Christianity (1:27).

On the other hand, poverty carries no guarantees of spirituality. A. W. Pink maintained: "Worry over poverty is as fatal to spiritual fruitfulness as is gloating over wealth."[6] Poverty more often makes people bitter rather than better. Christian commitment does not flourish in the nation's slums. Both poverty and affluence must be sanctified at Christ's feet. Neither one carries an automatic bless-ing or a damnation.

Honor for the Dishonorable? (2:6-7)

Christians contradict their calling when they fawn over the rich people and ignore the poor persons. James exposed the inconsis-tency of favoring the affluent and humiliating the poor. James's readers had "dishonored the poor man" (2:6). They failed to give the poor man the respect or grant him the weight that he deserved. James stated: "You humiliate the poor" or, "You insult the poor" (Moffatt).[7] In addition to the seating problem (Jas. 2:2-3), the early church humiliated the poor in other ways.

James fumed at his readers' contradictory behavior. The rich people whom they courted oppressed, exploited, and wrongfully sued Christians. Worse than that, they blasphemed Jesus' name. James leveled three charges against the non-Christian rich: (1) They oppressed the Christians because they were poor, Christian, or both. (2) They legally persecuted believers. (3) They blas-phemed Christ.

Moffatt translated James's statement: "The [unbelieving, v. 7] rich . . . lord it over you" (2:6). Such godless, affluent people dom-inated and exploited the Christians who courted their favor. James's word had a long Old Testament history that referred to the wealthy people's exploiting the poor. Ezekiel insisted that individ-uals were responsible for the poor. This included their return-ing the collateral, feeding the hungry, clothing the unclad, and refusing to charge interest (Ezek. 18:7-8). Amos cried out against the brutish urban women of Samaria. They oppressed the poor by hounding their husbands to provide an ever higher standard of living by exploiting the needy (Amos 4:1). Amos even accosted those who could not wait for "church" to be over so they could resume oppressive tactics (Amos 8:4-6). Just as Amos did, James judged Christians who sided with those who oppressed believers. For James, this was little short of siding with the devil.

"The [unbelieving, v. 7] rich . . . drag you into court" (2:6). Those to whom James's readers gave the best seats in the house returned the favor by dragging the Christians into court. On the pretext of trumped-up civil or criminal charges, the secular rich exploited poor believers. James probably had in mind cases that involved wages, debts, rent, or property. In the local synagogue-courts, the rich unjustly snatched away what little the Christians had.

Behind all the rich people's actions rested a religious motive. James saved the worse accusation until the last. The grasping materialists were guilty of a gross evil. James asked: "Is it not they who blaspheme that honorable name which was invoked over you?" (2:7). His question called for a Yes answer. The rich people spoke irreverently of Jesus. One can imagine that rich Jewish un-

believers angrily denounced Christians as the followers of a cursed criminal. Even in the early Christian assemblies, Christ's enemies probably stood to say, "'Jesus be cursed'" (1 Cor. 12:3). Yet James's readers were giving those people the best seats and were insulting the Christian poor!

Although James did not mention Jesus' name, he wrote of "the honorable name" (2:7). The word translated **honorable** means *beautiful, attractive, noble,* and *good.* Often, that beautiful name was all poor Christians possessed. Robert E. Lee "was approached after the Civil War by the managers of the infamous Louisiana Lottery. He sat in his old rocking-chair, crutches at his side, and listened to their proposition. He couldn't believe his ears; he asked them to repeat it, thinking that he couldn't have heard them aright. They said they wanted no money from him; all they wanted was the use of his name, and for that they would make him rich. Lee straightened up in his chair, buttoned his old grey tunic about him, and thundered, 'Gentlemen, I lost my home in the war. I lost my fortune in the war. I lost everything in the war except my name. My name is not for sale, and if you fellows don't get out of here I'll break this crutch over your heads.'"[8] For some, a good name is all that they have left. James believed that Christians would respond to an attack on Jesus' name. When he wrote that the rich blasphemed Jesus' name, he expected that his statement would motivate his readers to a high degree. More than one's own name, one must seek to honor His name.

All or Nothing (2:8-13)

God's law applies to all people equally. James called attention to the unity and impartiality of the divine law. The law of love mandates concern for everybody, not just those who are considered to be somebodies. To break God's law at one point breaks it altogether, for God's law is a unity. God will not judge Christians on the basis of minute commandments but on the basis of whether a life shows love. The person who refuses to give mercy on the human level will receive no mercy on the divine level.

The King of Laws: The Law of the King (2:8)
Sometimes, James wrote as if someone had interrupted him with an objection. Then, he responded with an argument. The ancient world called this the "diatribe" style. In verse 8, James imagined

an objection to his rebuke about partiality. Someone may have argued: *You have to love your rich enemies as well as your poor neighbors. I have to show deference to the rich man to keep God's law.* This ploy tried to sidestep the real issue. The objector presented a pretext to excuse himself. The devil can quote Scriptures. Today, one would say that James's objector hid behind the Bible.

James responded by agreeing with the priority of love. However, his response contains a degree of irony. My paraphrase would read: *If you really intended to keep the royal law perfectly, . . . you are doing well.* James knew that they did not intend to apply the law of love equally.

According to James, " 'You shall love your neighbor as yourself' " is the "royal law" (2:8). On Tuesday before Jesus' Friday crucifixion, a lawyer asked Him about the great Commandment. The Jews enjoyed debating about the Commandments. The great rabbis usually ranked them in importance. Jesus responded that love for God and love for neighbor topped all laws. Indeed, those commandments summarized "all the law and the prophets" (Matt. 22:34-40). Jesus had no argument from the Jews when He placed love for God first. Daily, the Jews repeated those words from Deuteronomy 6:4-9. They even bound them on their arms, wore them between their eyes, and inscribed them on their doorposts. But Jesus elevated a more obscure command from Leviticus 19:18 and made it a parallel command to the demand to love God. Regardless of how much people claim to love God, they do not do so unless they love their neighbors.

What did James mean by "the royal law"? Perhaps, he meant that it is the king of all laws. Paul flatly stated: "He who loves his neighbor has fulfilled the law" (Rom. 13:8). Elsewhere, he insisted: "The whole law is fulfilled in one word, 'You shall love your neighbor as yourself' " (Gal. 5:14). If believers master this, they have mastered everything that God demands. If they fail at this point, they have failed at every point. The law of love for one's neighbor is pivotal.

"The royal law" also can mean the law of the King. Christians recognize Jesus as God's King Messiah. In His inaugural sermon, Jesus openly claimed to fulfill the Old Testament law (Matt. 5:17). To pander to the rich while insulting the poor ignores Jesus' law. In His kingdom, love for neighbor is kingdom law. The neighbor is anyone on any of life's roads who needs help (Luke 10:25-37).

This generation stresses "back-to-basics." Nothing is more basic than the "royal law." Frustrated, angry Christian workers contradict their work. Football coach Vince Lombardi was fanatical about basics. Once, his Green Bay Packers were defeated by an inferior team. At the team meeting, the players had no idea what to expect. Lombardi gritted his teeth and stared holes through one man after another. Finally, he spoke: "'OK, we go back to basics this morning. . . .' Holding a football high enough for all to see, he continued to yell: 'Gentlemen, this is a football!'"[9] That is like telling a piano player, "This is middle C." It is like telling an artist, "This is a paintbrush." Yet, countless Christians and churches need to go back to basics in just that simple way. Business meetings that become verbal brawls, committee meetings that erupt with anger, and Christians who are too busy to stop for a neighbor contradict the "royal law." Christ's people need to get back to basics!

God's Law: Handle with Care (2:9-11)

In shops that deal with delicate china and glass, one often sees the familiar warning: "If you drop it, you bought it." How many objects one breaks makes no difference; to break anything is to pay for the broken item. The high value of precious objects demands payment in full when the objects are broken. The high value of God's law also demands payment in full when it is broken—even part of it.

James wrote that partiality marked one as a spiritual rebel. "Transgressors" are those who step over the line in rebellion against God (2:9). Perhaps James's readers considered their partiality toward the rich to be harmless. James deepened the blackness of their prejudice by listing it with murder and adultery (2:11). What is worse, such partiality made them guilty of breaking God's entire law.

God's law is a unit. Today, the laws of our land brand one a criminal regardless of which law is broken. To break God's law at one point reveals an attitude that could break it at any point. The character of every rebellious act reveals an inner disposition that can rebel even more. James bluntly stated the case: "'Whoever keeps the whole law but fails in one point has become guilty of all of it'" (2:10). People cannot despise the poor and keep God's favor any more than they can commit murder and still please Him.

James certainly did not mean that every sin is the same in its consequences. As Curtis Vaughan observed: "James is not dealing with the extent and degree of guilt, but with its reality. Some sins obviously are more heinous in the sight of God than others."[10] For example, adultery which actually is committed devastates far more than lust devastates. Lust consumes the lustful person. The act of adultery involves the adulterer, his partner in shame, and the betrayed spouses of both persons. Yet, Jesus seemed to attach equal guilt before God to the thoughts of lust and to the acts of lust (Matt. 5:28). Open adultery and hidden lust are unequal in their human consequences; but, they are equal in their damning guilt before God.

Believers must see God's law in the context of relationships. God gave His law as principles for guiding His relationship to His people. When persons break a single item of God's law, they violate their relationship with God. A son may ruin his relationship with his father by petty disobedience or by outright physical injury. In both instances, the father-son relationship has been fractured. Behind James's statement stands the character of the relationship between God and persons. Anything that harms that relationship overturns God's whole law.

Christ did not die merely for sins, but for sin. In His death, Christ reunified by obedience to His father what people broke in disobedience. In disobeying part of the Law, people broke all of it. Christ's death paid the penalty for the whole broken Law. Persons who have broken all of God's law now can know all of God's righteousness through Christ. God's grace more than covered people's guilt and disobedience. Thank God for the truth that John Henry Jowett grasped: "Law says 'Do,' grace says, 'Done.'"[11]

Here Comes the Judge (2:12-13)

In light of God's stern requirements, every believer should live daily in the light of the final judgment. James's choice of words suggests a certainty and a fixed date for God's coming judgment. Every believer will be judged by the "law of liberty" (2:12). That is the law that Moses transmitted and that Christ interpreted. Those who have shown no mercy to others will find no mercy with God. James must have remembered Jesus' Beatitude: "'Blessed are the merciful, for they shall obtain mercy'" (Matt. 5:7). The opposite also is true: Cursed are the merciless, for they shall find no mercy. James had in mind particularly the partiality that insulted the poor (2:2-4). Jesus' parable of the unjust steward vividly portrays God's judgment against merciless behavior. God forgives enormous sins. However, He will not excuse a lack of mercy (Matt. 18:21-35).

If persons stand on their rights with others, God will stand on

His rights. The individual who is all claim, demand, and law will meet a God who is all claim, demand, and law. As Thomas Adams quaintly put it: "That which a man spits against heaven shall fall back on his own face."[12]

Lessons for Life from 2:1-13

Take immediate action to identify and to remedy partiality in individual and church life.—You should take inventory of all relationships quietly and slowly. The neighborhood, club, business, and social scene should fall under this inventory. Do you secretly consider yourself to be above some acquaintances and beneath others? Do you turn your back on a person of lesser status in order to court the favor of a person whom you think is important?

Make the church a place where everyone truly is welcome.— When new members are presented, do not judge them by age, dress, or physical appearance. In light of James's stern warnings, believers should go out of their way to welcome those who are not likely to receive a warm welcome.

Believers should be involved directly and personally with the poor.—No one honestly can read the Bible and escape this responsibility. No amount of indirect contributions to church or charity can substitute for personal contact and concern for the poor. Where are the poor in your daily life-style? At what times and in what ways can you help the poor while you maintain their dignity?

Christians must not let church work become so exhausting that they fail to love their neighbors.—Everyone is familiar with the tired, tense church member whose life becomes a contradiction of Christian love. Make sure that the church's work truly is Christ's work.

---

1. G. B. F. Hallock and M. K. W. Heicher, *Doran's Ministers Manual* (New York: Harper & Brothers, 1941), p. 396.

2. James Hardy Ropes, *A Critical and Exegetical Commentary on the Epistle of St. James*, "Ethiopic Statutes of the Apostles" (Edinburgh: T. & T. Clark, reprinted 1954), p. 191.

3. John Scanzoni, "The Man with the Gold-Ringed Finger," *Eternity*, August, 1963, p. 13.

4. Ibid., p. 12.

5. *Christian Century*, November 10, 1982, p. 1126.

6. John Blanchard, *Gathered Gold* (Bath, England: The Pitman Press, 1984), p. 217.

7. From *The Bible: a New Translation* by James A. R. Moffatt. Copyright © 1935 by Harper and Row, Publishers, Inc. Used by permission. Subsequent quotations are marked Moffatt.

8. J. Wallace Hamilton, *Ride the Wild Horses* (Westwood, New Jersey: Fleming H. Revel, 1952), p. 122.

9. Charles R. Swindoll, *Growing Strong in the Seasons of Life* (Portland, Oregon: Multnomah Press, 1983), p. 373.

10. Curtis Vaughan, *A Study Guide: James* (Grand Rapids, Mich.: Zondervan Pub. House, 1969), p. 53.

11. Blanchard, p. 181

12. Ibid., 176.

Personal Learning Activities

1. According to Dr. Gregory, the word "faith" in James 2:1 means (select the correct answer from the list):

    ____(1) A body of doctrine. ____(3) Personal trust in Christ.

    ____(2) Faithfulness. ____(4) Blind confidence.

2. James warned that _____ threatened the fabric of the church. (Choose the proper response from the list.)

    (1) Immorality (3) Partiality

    (2) Lawlessness (4) Politics

3. Probably, the early church consisted largely of middle- to upper-middle-class people. ____True ____False

4. James called the demand, "You shall love your neighbor as yourself," the _____.

Answers:

1. (3); 2. (3); 3. False; 4. Royal law.

4
A Faith
that Works
James 2:14-26

A diamond! The word *diamond* implies value, durability, and brilliance. A diamond began by God's creative initiative in the hidden places under the earth's surface. In a mystery that human effort cannot duplicate, heat and pressure transformed carbon into a diamond. In 1955, General Electric synthesized a poor, industrial-grade diamond. That took 1,500,000 pounds of pressure per square inch at a temperature of 5,000 degrees Fahrenheit. Similarly, at God's intiative, He makes salvation available by faith. What He has provided is beyond human effort. He worked that salvation in the heat and pressure of Calvary. People cannot do that. Salvation is God's greatest creation.

On the other hand, no one knows a diamond's genuineness until an expert examines it for the "four C's" that determine the value of every stone: carat, cut, clarity, and color.

Paul and James wrote about saving faith and authenticating works. Paul's interest fastened on the beginning of faith. Just as a diamond originates in the hidden mystery of God's initiative, faith begins in God's saving act. However, James focused on the continuing evidence of faith. Just as a jeweler examines a stone for evidence, James examined professed faith for marks of reality. Like a miner who discovered a diamond and wondered at its origin, Paul wrote of faith's origin in God's grace. Like a jeweler appraising a stone, James looked at the works which vindicate faith.

The Critical Concern (2:14)

Every sincere seeker confronts a crucial concern: What is the nature of faith that ultimately saves at God's final judgment? In 2:14, James held a written dialogue with himself, his readers, and a straw man. "What does it profit, my brethren, if a man says he has faith but has not works? Can his faith save him?" (2:14). James's interrupter claimed to have genuine faith. By this, he must have meant the basic attitude toward a doctrine that made one a Christian. Sometimes, the word *faith* emphasizes warm personal trust in Christ. At other times, faith signifies the body of beliefs that a Christian holds. James's straw man claimed to have habitual, personal trust in the right doctrine of faith.

James made an additional observation and asked two questions. The observation was: This man had a wordy but workless faith. Words without deeds marked his "faith." First, James questioned the value of such a profession: "What does it profit?" Alternatively, this means: What use is it? Or, What good is it? The phrase in Greek implies: It is no use at all. Wordy but workless faith is worthless.

James's second question looked ahead to the judgment: "Can his faith save him?" My paraphrase reads: *Can such a faith as this acquit him in the final judgment?* The question demands a sharp, unyielding, No! In the final appraisal, this diamond will be revealed to be an imitation which is made of worthless glass. Faith based on no more than words and ritual will be unmasked as counterfeit.

James and Paul: Friends, not Foes

In every generation, an apparent difficulty baffles students of James. Superficially, James seemed to challenge Paul on the relationship between faith and works in salvation. This apparent difficulty may be seen by comparing Paul's words, "For we hold that a man is justified by faith apart from works of law" (Rom. 3:28), with James 2:14, 24: "What does it profit, my brethren, if a man says he has faith but has not works? Can his faith save him?" "You see that a man is justified by works and not by faith alone."

Sometimes, sincere readers have misunderstood James. These include Martin Luther. He called James "an epistle of straw" and without evangelical character.[1] Luther's Reformation cried: "Salvation by faith alone." Reacting against the Roman church's works-oriented salvation, Luther misunderstood James. Others continue to misunderstand him. Five crucial facts clear up this disturbing misunderstanding: (1) Paul and James believed in salvation by God's grace alone through faith; (2) the remainder of the New Testament agrees with James that good works give evidence of faith's genuineness; (3) Paul insisted that faith always produces good works; (4) Paul and James used the key words *works* and *faith* with significant differences in meaning; (5) Paul and James fought different opponents, not one another. These five facts deserve more detailed study.

1. James believed that God's grace grants salvation just as Paul believed. James wrote: "Receive with meekness the implanted word, which is able to save your souls" (1:21). God graciously implants the saving Word while the believer waits in meek receptivity. In James's section on repentance (4:1-10), he wrote that God "gives grace to the humble" (4:6). God's grace comes to those who humble themselves in repentance. A recognized authority on James, James Hardy Ropes, insisted: "He [James] has no idea of disparaging faith, which he everywhere assumes as present and which he highly values. His point is that faith and works are inseparable in any properly constituted Christian life, and he argues this clearly and effectively."[2]

2. The remainder of the New Testament agrees with James on the necessity of obedience as proof of real faith. Jesus warned: "'Not every one who says to me, "Lord, Lord," shall enter the kingdom of heaven, but he who does the will of my Father who is in heaven'" (Matt. 7:21). James and Jesus agreed that verbal profession is not enough. Real faith works. Jesus insisted that final judgment would include the same concerns that James repeated: food for the hungry, clothes for the naked, and help for the helpless. These will be evidences on which the reality of professed faith will be judged (Matt. 25:31-46). John the Baptist stood solidly with Jesus and James. He insisted that a real relationship with God must "'bear fruits that befit repentance'" (Luke 3:7). John the Baptist insisted on exactly the same works that James did for proof of real salvation: clothes for the naked, food for the hungry, and no extortion of the helpless. (See Luke 3:10-14; Jas. 2:15-16; 5:4-6.)

3. Paul agreed with James that faith produces a radical change in one's deeds. After Paul's strongest statement on salvation by grace through faith alone, he insisted that saving faith does work:

"We are his workmanship, created in Christ Jesus for good works, which God prepared beforehand, that we should walk in them" (Eph. 2:10). In grace, God purposes a new creation so that good works may result. From eternity, God prepared a road of good deeds on which every believer invariably will walk. No exception exists. By God's divine decree, faith works.

4. James and Paul used the same words with different meanings. This should not surprise anyone. The English language does this often. Take the word *rest*. If a friend says, *I got some rest last night*, the statement means a brief period of refreshing sleep. If a doctor says, *You need more rest*, that indicates a much longer, more serious period of relaxation. If a funeral director tells a caller, *We will lay him to rest today*, that indicates a longer period of rest! The meaning obviously depends on the context.

In the same way, Paul and James used the words *works*, *faith*, and *justify* with some important differences. For Paul, the word *works* included especially the ceremonial law of Judaism: ritual washings, dietary laws, feast days, and so on. By "works of the law" (Rom. 3:20), Paul meant human activities by which a person attempts to earn salvation. On the other hand, when James spoke of works, he meant moral deeds of love which result from living faith. For Paul, **faith** usually meant *warm, personal trust in Jesus*. In James 2:14, **faith** may mean *intellectual agreement to a creed*, not effective, saving trust in Christ. The word *justify* will be discussed in the treatment of 2:24.

5. Finally, Paul and James stood back to back fighting different opponents, not face to face fighting one another. Paul opposed legalistic believers. By keeping the law, these people sought to obligate God to save them. James fought lax believers. These persons claimed that a mere verbal confession of faith saved a person. Paul and James literally fought enemies coming from two directions.

On October 25, 1983, the elite Ranger division parachuted onto the new Point Salinas airstrip on the tiny island of Granada. Such an act presents one of the most daring and dangerous situations a soldier can face. Enemy fire bursts from all directions at once. Immediately, the infantry employed the "buddy system." Fighting back to back, two infantrymen cover themselves until the objective is taken. In the same way, James and Paul fought the early, great battle of the church with the "buddy system." As brothers in Christ, they covered each other and all generations of believers by establishing the true nature of saving faith that works.

A Concrete Case (2:15-17)

Someone may say: Enough theology! What does James want me to do? In a December, 1980, letter to friends, George Sweeting, President of Moody Bible Institute, shared an experience that he had with one of his students:

> Just recently, one of our students—I'll call him John—was returning to the campus from the nearby YMCA where he had been playing basketball. He was wearing his gym clothes and his "warm-up" suit and carried his street clothes and shoes under his arm.
>
> As he hurried down the street, a poorly dressed man stopped him and asked him for some money. John asked him why he needed the money, and the man said he was hungry. So John invited the man to join him for a hamburger at a nearby restaurant.
>
> As they ate together, John noticed the tattered and torn clothes he was wearing, and his worn-out shoes; so John gave the man his street shoes. John also shared the way of salvation with the man and told him how he could invite Jesus Christ into his heart and have eternal life. They prayed together and after a while John left to return to the campus.
>
> But as he left the restaurant, John was stopped again . . . this time by an elderly lady standing outside the restaurant waiting for a bus. She had been watching John inside the restaurant. She asked him, "Why did you help that man? People just don't do that anymore." As John began to share his testimony with her, they were so busy talking, the lady missed her bus; so John offered to carry her shopping packages and take her a few blocks to another bus stop where she would not have to wait so long. As they walked and talked, the lady was so moved by what she had seen and heard, she told John that she would like to accept Christ. Before she got on the bus, she had prayed with John and invited Christ into her heart and life.
>
> As I think of John's experience, I remember the words of one of my favorite gospel songs: "They will know we are Christians by our love." Because of John's love for others and his eagerness to introduce people to Jesus Christ, the world became a better place for two people that day.[3]

What church could not use an evangelism program like that?

Yet, James described a believer who reacted differently from John. Some interpreters believe that James told a parable in 2:15-16. This little slice of life gives such a self-evident, crass example that it would be clear to all. On the other hand, James may have reported an event that he saw. Perhaps a sanctimonious church official hurried someone out of the meeting place: "'Blessings on you, keep warm, eat until you have plenty'" (2:16b, Williams).[4]

James's word *if* (2:15) suggests a hypothetical case. The needy person was a brother or a sister in the Christian community. Curt Christians gave the needy person a seat on the floor by their footstools (2:3). The individual appeared in rags and starving. **Ill-clad** translates a term that can mean *stark naked*. Here, it probably meant *without an outer garment*. The person lived at a subsistence level. All of this underlined the urgency of the need.

The curt Christians' response shocks even today's reader: "'Good luck to you, keep yourselves warm, and have plenty to eat'" (2:16, NEB).[5] How were these words spoken? That they were spoken in contempt or mockery is unlikely. They probably were spoken with a well-meaning smile. But the problem was just that: The words were only words. "Go in peace" reflects the common Jewish parting word **shalom.** In essence, the situation is like someone's telling the poor: *You have had spiritual food and are clothed in Christ's righteousness. Good-bye.*

The advice "be warmed and filled" (2:16) can suggest effort on the poor persons' part: "Find warmth and food for yourselves" (2:16).[6] Or, the words may suggest a general passive attitude: *Let somebody else do it, but not me.* The words bark a command which indicates a habitual, heartless attitude on the speaker's part. The word *filled* is laden with irony. It referred to animals that gorged themselves to the point of satiation, as cattle in a feed lot. The needy person only craved a morsel to sustain life for a day.

"What does it profit?" (2:16) began this section of James (2:14a). Will the poor offer heartfelt gratitude for your good wishes? Will God affirm your saying that you have faith? Certainly, such worthless words do not fill empty stomachs. Just as certainly, such fake faith yields no spiritual profit for the sham believer.

Do you think that James's opinion is peculiar? Then compare the words of his fellow-apostle, John: "If any one has the world's goods and sees his brother in need, yet closes his heart against him, how does God's love abide in him?" (1 John 3:17). Such a heartless Christian knows nothing of God's love. What an irony that professed believers can spend a lifetime running from meeting to committee, convention to seminar, preacher to lecturer, and still demonstrate fake faith! The priest and the Levite conveniently "passed by on the other side" (Luke 10:31-32). The rush of busy religion often overlooks needs at its feet. Jesus promised no salvation, much less a reward, to those whose faith knows nothing but religious busyness without concrete compassion.

Paul Cho's church in Seoul, Korea, is the largest congregation in the world. Recently, 210,000 people attended the seven Sunday services. When he dismisses services, Cho tells his people to find someone in the streets of Seoul and to help them. They do just that. Some help young mothers carry groceries up the stairs. Others help old people onto public transportation. The city knows that Cho's church does not practice invisible faith, but concrete Christianity. No amount of hype, promotion, or slogans ever will substitute for such living. The church that practices it can explode. The church that ignores it will die.

A Crucial Correction (2:18)

In dramatic form, James presented an objection: "But some one will say, "'You have faith and I have works'" (2:18). Some debate surrounds the meaning of this objection. James's opponent may have stated this in a flippant way. Perhaps the statement could be paraphrased: *You theologians can debate about faith and works all you desire. Some folks are doers, and some are believers. We're all trying to get to the same place.* Shortly before writing these words, I tried to witness to a young man in a hotel. Formerly, he had been a Baptist; but he had been converted to the Islamic faith. When I confronted him with the uniqueness of Jesus, he dodged the discussion with the same words: "We're all trying to get to the same place."

More likely, however, James's opponent spoke in a hostile or angry voice. Some interpreters understand the objector to distinguish between faith and works as if the two were separate spiritual gifts. Some people would have the gift of faith, and others would have the gift of works. Paul did list a special spiritual gift of faith (1 Cor. 12:9). However, by that gift he did not mean saving faith that is common to all believers. Rather, he referred to a special gift of extraordinary or miracle-working faith. Saving faith and Christian works do not exist separately as two spiritual gifts. In every believer, the two are as inseparable as the spirit and the body (Jas. 2:26).

At least one scholar detected a church-wide misunderstanding behind James 2:18. Bo Reicke suggested that some believers in the early church tried to assist Gentile conversion by suggesting that "faith" was enough; deeds were not necessary. Perhaps such church members told potential converts that "faith" alone would suffice; deeds were not necessary. Earlier, the Pharisees made a separation between Jews who could fulfill the law's demands fully and those who could not. Since they had divided the law of Moses into 613 lesser commandments, many people could not even remember all of the commands. Thus, some members of Pharisaic groups accepted vicarious responsibility to perform good works on behalf of the many who would not! In this trade-off, some members had faith and others had works.[7]

James's reply admits no false division between faith and works: "Show me your faith apart from your works, and I by my works will show you my faith" (2:18). James considered his opponent to be wrong. Only Christian deeds show real faith. Can one display faith in any other way? How much would a square foot of faith weigh? What size or color is faith? Such questions indicate the absurdity of claiming faith without works. Faith is an inward attitude toward God; without Christian deeds, it remains invisible.

For example, millions of Americans exercise each week in order to gain "aerobic points." Around thirty points that one gains every week should indicate good cardiovascular fitness. Yet, has anyone ever seen an aerobic point? How much does one weigh? What shape is it? Such questions sound absurd. One only sees an aerobic point in the exercise of jogging, cycling, swimming, and so on. One glimpses the reality of an aerobic point only in the physical exertion. An aerobic point has no independent existence apart from the exercise which demonstrates it. Likewise, faith never stands alone without the works that demonstrate it. God saves by faith only, but faith never is alone.

A Confused Confession (2:19-20)

Those who insisted on faith without works mouthed the most orthodox of creeds: "God is one" (2:19). To confess God's existence and unity is the foundation of all Jewish and Christian belief. From the days of Moses, every Hebrew repeated the great confession of Deuteronomy 6:4-5: "'Hear, O Israel: The Lord our God is one Lord; and you shall love the Lord your God with all your heart, and with all your soul, and with all your might.'" These two

verses were so famous that they were given a name, the **Shema.**
That is the Hebrew word for *hear,* the first word in verse 4. The
words of the **Shema** literally were worn next to the heart and in a
box on the forehead. Jews taught them to their children and placed
them in boxes beside their front door.

The value that the Jews attached to the words of the **Shema**
reached almost superstitious proportions. For example, Jewish
tradition taught: "'Whosoever prolongs the utterance of the word
One (Deut. 6:4) shall have his days and years prolonged to him.'"[8]
Just to utter the word *One* supposedly prolonged life. The famous
Rabbi Akiba faced a martyr's death. At the end of his final prayer,
he recited the **Shema.** His last words were: "'Hear, O Israel, the
Lord thy God is *one.*'" According to Jewish legend, a voice from
heaven was heard: "'Blessed art thou, for thy soul and the word
One left thy body together.'" To maintain to the end this verbal
confession virtually guaranteed a blessing at death.[9]

Evidently, those who insisted on mouthing the creed "God is
one" considered that merely saying it was enough. James certainly
did not discount the validity or necessity of that confession. Every
believer must make it. God's unity and existence are no less a
Christian than a Jewish confession. (See 1 Cor. 8:4; Eph. 4:6;
1 Thess. 1:8.) For pagans turning from the worship of many gods
to Christ, to confess God's oneness was essential. Jesus called it
the great Commandment of the Law. The early and greatest creed
of the church, the Nicene Creed, presented God's unity in its first
article. James in no way minimized the confession of God's unity.
He wrote: "You do well" (2:19). He did not mean that this confession exhausted all that Christians must believe. Christians believe this and much more. To confess God's unity is necessary, but
it is not enough. The Christian must confess Jesus' lordship as the
only begotten Son of God. The believer must add to that confession a life of beautiful deeds to demonstrate the truth of the
confession.

Confirming Case Studies (2:21-25)

Great theological truths clamor for demonstration in daily life.
One needs a concrete incarnation of truth as much as theological
information about truth. For that reason, James gave two case studies to show that saving faith always produces godly works. His
examples represent two opposite extremes of humanity: Abraham

the godly patriarch and Rahab the godless prostitute. Both of these Old Testament figures demonstrated faith that works.

A Godly Patriarch (2:21-24)

No one ever questioned Abraham's faith. For Jews and Gentiles, he stands as the embodiment of a life of faith. Indeed, Paul gave him the highest compliment in the family of faith: He is "the father of all who believe" (Rom. 4:11). For the Gentiles no less than the Jews, Abraham stands as the head of God's family of believing children. Abraham is the first man whose faith explicitly is mentioned in the Bible (Gen. 15:6). Whereas others before him did believe, the first specific act of faith was attributed to Abraham. He formed a good case study for James, because no one questioned Abraham's faith.

Steve Allen hosted an interesting television show, a meeting of great minds. The format presented an imaginary situation in which men and women from different centuries and various walks of life sat around the same conference table. Perhaps Alexander the Great, Woodrow Wilson, Florence Nightingale, and Julius Caesar would all discuss a common topic. Because they lived centuries apart, the show was amusing but actually impossible. What if one could seat Abraham, Moses, David, and Paul around the same table? Three of them quickly would agree that the fourth one was the greatest of all when it came to a life of faith. They would identify Abraham as the greatest of all at the point of faith.

James used Abraham as the perfect test case by pointing out two dramatic moments in Abraham's life. James first pointed to the moment when Abraham revealed the reality of his faith by attempting to sacrifice Isaac (2:21). Next, James indicated the time earlier in Abraham's life when the patriarch first trusted God; therefore, God pronounced him righteous (2:23). James reversed the order of the events in time in order to stress Abraham's works. Keep in mind these two events and their order in time.

God Pronounced Abraham Righteous (Gen. 15:6; Jas. 2:23)
Abraham Shown to Be Righteous Through Works (Gen. 22; Jas. 2:21)

Keep in mind that the first event took place forty years before the second one. Initially, God *justified* Abraham by pronouncing him righteous. Finally, Abraham was *justified* (shown to be upright) by his works. An examination of these two events that took place forty years apart clarifies the two meanings of the word *jus-*

tify. Also, that God saved Abraham on the basis of faith alone becomes clear. Following that, Abraham's obedient deeds vindicated that grace.

Initially, the moon-worshiping Mesopotamian Abram heard God's voice and abandoned Ur. He started west with God at age seventy-five. How God spoke to him, no one knows. Was in it a dream by night, a vision by day, or an audible voice? What matters is Abraham's faith response to God's call. Abraham peered up at the sky where a million pinpricks of light looked like diamonds against black velvet. God promised him that his offspring would be more numerous than the stars. Abraham "believed the Lord; and he reckoned it to him as righteousness" (Gen. 15:6). The wording implies that God wrote it down in His book (accounted) that Abraham was righteous. Paul rejoiced in this great truth. He repeated it in Romans 4:3,22, citing Genesis 15:6 twice. God declared Abraham to be righteous on the basis of belief, apart from his works. Paul concluded that God justifies all people apart from their works (Rom. 4:5). James heartily agreed with Paul that Abraham's initial experience with God was justification by faith alone (Jas. 2:23).

Years passed before God gave Isaac, the son of promise. Probably, when Isaac reached nine or ten years of age, God gave a startling command to Abraham. "'Take your son, your only son Isaac, whom you love, and go to the land of Moriah, and offer him there as a burnt offering upon one of the mountains of which I shall tell you'" (Gen. 22:2). Who could forget the gripping story that followed? Abraham tried to offer his son as a sacrifice in absolute obedience to God's command. Only God's intervention kept Abraham from the act. James insisted that this act of obedience justified Abraham. James used the word in a different way from Paul. **Justify** can mean to *pronounce or make righteous*. James in 2:23 and Paul in Romans 4 used the word in that sense. But **justify** also can mean *to show upright* or *to vindicate as righteous*. Williams rendered James 2:21: "Was not our forefather Abraham shown to be upright by his good deeds, namely, by offering Isaac his son upon the altar?"

Wiersbe caught the essence of this truth: "By faith, he was justified *before God* and his righteousness declared; by works he was justified *before men* and his righteousness demonstrated."[10] "God pronounced Abraham righteous and recorded his righteousness. Over twenty-five years later, Abraham's works justified on earth what had been announced in heaven.

For James, the combination of faith plus works yields a synergism. That word does not belong to normal, daily vocabulary. If you consult a dictionary, you will find that a synergism results when two or more things combine. In a synergism, they combine so that the whole is more than the sum of its parts. For example, ordinary table salt consists of two chemical elements, sodium and chlorine. By itself, sodium is a highly reactive, poisonous element. Chlorine also is poisonous and reactive. Yet, bringing the two together yields sodium chloride (ordinary table salt). Not only is it not poisonous, it is necessary for life. In a simliar way, faith that stands alone is deadly (2:17). Merely to mouth a creed poisons one's religious life. On the other hand, works alone are just as deadly. The arrogant attempt to work one's way to God produces futility (Rom. 4). Yet the synergism of a faith that works yields spiritual life.

James pointed out the faith-work synergism: "Surely you can see that faith was at work in his actions, and that by these actions the integrity of his faith was fully proved" (2:22, NEB). Work had a complementary relationship to Abraham's faith, not a supplementary relationship. Faith was expressed dramatically in good deeds. Abraham's works cooperated with his faith. He was not saved by faith plus works; he was saved by a faith that worked. Each step of obedience in Abraham's long life strengthened his faith.

A Godless Prostitute (2:25)

James deliberately designed the greatest conceivable contrast to the godly patriarch Abraham. Abraham was a Jew; Rahab was a Gentile. He was a man; she was a woman. What is more, she was a weak, erring woman—a prostitute. Yet, Hebrews 11:31 designates her as a woman of faith. She confessed her faith in God clearly: "'The Lord your God is he who is God in heaven above and on earth beneath'" (Josh. 2:11). But Rahab did not merely mouth a creed. She took elaborate precaution to lodge Israel's spies and to send them off in a safe direction. (See Jas. 2:25.) As simple as her faith was, it was a faith that worked. Her faith acted immediately, and with some degree of risk for her. By using examples so different, James implied that all who claim faith must show that faith by deeds. Rahab's acting faith earned her a place among Jesus' ancestors (Matt. 1:5).

A Climactic Conclusion (2:26)

The relationship between faith and works is like that between the body and the spirit. Without the spirit, the body is a corpse. Without works, faith is dead. Wordy but workless faith is worthless.

Lessons for Life from James 2:14-26

Christians always should be narrowing the gap between what they know and what they do.—They may keep log books of sermons or Bible studies that they attend. On one side, they may write the subject and on the other enter the definite, concrete living that the message motivated.

Believers need to discover the helpless people in their communities.—Jesus stated clearly that working faith meets life's basic needs. No believer should feel exempt from feeding the hungry persons and clothing the ill-clad people. Where are these people in your community? What contact do you have with them?

Check the balance between words and deeds in Christian liv-

ing.—When believers are long on words and short on deeds of love, a serious imbalance exists. Some need to confess less and to do more.

Does what you confess at church match what you live at home?—John Bunyan's character, Mr. Talkative, was a saint at church but a devil at home. The home is the crucible of Christian living. No one can fool people at home for long. Faith that does not do loving deeds at home is questionable.

_____

1. Sophie Laws, *A Commentary on the Epistle of James* (New York: Harper & Row, Publishers, 1980), p. 1.

2. James Hardy Ropes, *A Critical and Exegetical Commentary on the Epistle of St. James* (Edinburgh: T. & T Clark, 1954), p. 35.

3. George Sweeting, letter used by permission.

4. From *The New Testament, a Translation in the Language of the People,* by Charles B. Williams. Copyright 1937 and 1966. Moody Press, Moody Bible Institute of Chicago. Used by permission. Subsequent quotations are marked Williams.

5. From *The New English Bible.* Copyright © The Delegates of the Oxford University Press and the Syndics of the Cambridge University Press, 1961, 1970. Reprinted by permission. Subsequent quotations are marked NEB.

6. Helen Barrett Montgomery, *Centenary Translation of the New Testament* (Chicago: The American Baptist Publication Society, 1924), p. 626.

7. Bo Reicke, *The Anchor Bible, The Epistles of James, Peter and Jude,* (Garden City, NY: Doubleday & Co., 1964), p. 33.

8. R. J. Knowling, *The Epistle of St. James* (London: Methuene Co., 1904), p. 57.

9. Ibid., p. 57.

10. Warren W. Wiersbe, *Be Mature* (Wheaton, Ill.: Victor Books, 1978, ninth printing 1982), p. 83.

Personal Learning Activities

1. James challenged Paul on the matter of the relationship between faith and works in salvation. ____ True ____ False
2. To James and to other New Testament writers, _____ is the proof of genuine faith. (Choose the correct answer from the list.)
   (1) Profession   (3) Obedience
   (2) Religious ritual   (4) Keeping the Law
3. Saving faith always will issue in (select the proper response from the list):
   ____(1) A sinless life.   ____(3) Automatic maturity.
   ____(2) Good works.   ____(4) Multiple spiritual gifts.

4. James contended that orthodox confession must be coupled with a life of beautiful deeds. ____ True ____ False
5. In presenting his case on faith and works, James used _____ and _____ as illustrations. (Choose the correct responses from the list.)

(1) Noah   (3) Ruth   (5) David
(2) Abraham   (4) Moses   (6) Rahab

Answers:

1. False; 2. (3); 3. (2); 4. True; 5. (2),(6).

5
Tame the Tongue
James 3:1-18

There is nothing more slippery or loose than the tongue.[1]
John Calvin

On a windswept hill in an old English churchyard stands a slate tombstone. The elements almost have erased the inscription, but one barely can make out the epitaph:

Beneath This Stone, a Lump of Clay,
   Lies Arabella Young,
Who, on the Twenty-fourth of May,
   Began to Hold Her Tongue.[2]

During that period, many tombstones bore statements of truth. What epitaph truthfully would state the case of our speech? Obviously, Arabella had difficulty taming her tongue.

James gave more attention to the dangers of the tongue than any other New Testament writer. He mentioned some aspect of speech in each chapter of his letter. James 2:14-26 pronounces judgment on separating faith and works. In no area is this more likely than in human speech. While Christians profess one thing with their speech, often they practice something quite different. Nothing is opened more by mistake than the mouth.

James's cautions about the tongue comprise one of the most vivid passages in the New Testament. He began with a warning about the tongue and the teacher (3:1-2). He continued with memorable illustrations of the tongue's disproportionate influence

(3:3-5). Selecting from the various levels of creation, he compared the tongue to fire, stains, beasts, and poison (3:6-8). He marveled at the tongue's contradictory behavior, unlike anything else in nature (3:9-12). Finally, he contrasted speech that was controlled by worldly wisdom to speech controlled by heavenly wisdom (3:13-18). James warned: Don't let your tongue be your undoing.

The Tongue and the Teacher (3:1-2)

Jewish culture prized the office of teacher beyond our ability to convey. The word **rabbi** meant *my great one*. To fear the rabbi-teacher was equated with fear of God. The student who argued with his rabbi argued with the Shekinah, God's presence. "'To speak with the teacher, to invite him to be the guest, to marry his daughter, Israel was taught to consider the highest honour. The young men were expected to count it their glory to carry the Rabbi's burdens, to bring his water, to load his ass.'"[3] Many Israelites of means wanted to be rabbis. To be a teacher meant position, power, and prestige.

One easily can see that mixed motives propelled men to seek the office of teacher. For that reason James warned: "My brothers, do not crowd in to be teachers" (3:1, Moffatt).[4] He prohibited the continuation of a danger that he had detected in the early church. The Jewish rabbi's prestige carried over to the Christian teacher. One must keep in mind the informal structure of the earliest churches. Paul indicated that the services were spontaneous affairs where anyone in the fellowship could stand and speak. At Corinth, virtually everyone had something to teach (1 Cor. 14:26). In such a situation, the seductive prestige of the teacher's office tempted many. James stated that not many of his readers should become teachers.

James gave an excellent reason for his warning: "You know that we who teach shall be judged with greater strictness" (3:1). James included himself in his warning. He, too, was a teacher. The final judgment will be more exacting for those who teach Christian truths.

John Calvin ascended a high pulpit in his Geneva church. He once stated that it would be better for him to fall and break his neck while climbing to the pulpit than to preach the truth without first applying it to his own life.[5]

Everyone acknowledges the contradiction of preachers who do

not practice what they preach. A doctor who neglects his health, an accountant who cannot balance his checkbook, or an attorney who is in trouble with the law contradict the things for which they stand. Likewise, Christian teachers who do not control their tongues contradict their teaching.

James did not imply that the tongue held the only possibility for sin. "We all stumble in many ways" (3:2, NASB).[6] All people trip up spiritually many times and in various ways. James included himself as he stated sin's universal and repetitive character. I have seen a great deal of embarrassing stumbling. I have witnessed brides stumble at the wedding altar, student preachers stumble walking into the pulpit, and a funeral attendant stumble into a grave. I have watched wide receivers of my *alma mater* stumble on the twenty-yard line with no one between them and the goal line. The human race is a stumbling race—spiritually and physically. Yet, humans are nowhere more apt to stumble than in their speech.

When persons can control the tongue, they can do anything that the Christian faith demands. "If any one makes no mistakes in what he says he is a perfect man, able to bridle the whole body also" (3:2). If Christians tame their tongues, they can control any passion of their bodies. The word *perfect* implies a full-grown person as compared with a child. Such a Christian will not be sinless, but he/she will have reached ripe, spiritual maturity in controlled speech. James alone used the word *bridle* in the New Testament (3:2; also 1:26). The word suggests the tongue's energetic willfulness. To tame the tongue requires the same strength of determination as breaking a wild horse. Wise individuals often desire to do the most difficult task first, leaving the easier task for later. In Christian living, one is wiser to start with the tongue. Victory there would indicate mature self-control and self-discipline.

Small but Strong (3:3-5)

The tongue is a small piece of muscle covered with mucous membrane. Do not let its size mislead you. According to James, it is tiny but terrible. He gave three vivid illustrations of things that are small but strong: (1) The small bit controls the great power of the horse; (2) the small rudder controls the significant direction of the ship; and (3) the small brushfire can destroy the great forest.

"If we put bits into the mouths of horses that they may obey us, we guide their whole bodies" (3:3). By controlling the mouth, the rider controls not only the horse's head but the whole horse. This illustration particularly suited James's direction of thought. If people can control their tongues, they can control their whole bodies (3:2). If one can control the bit in a horse's mouth, he/she can control the entire horse. The power of a bit in the horse's mouth is enormous. One of the largest horses ever recorded was a purebred Belgian stallion named Brooklyn Supreme. The horse weighed 3200 pounds and stood 19.2 hands tall. He died at age twenty on a farm in Callender, Iowa, more than thirty years ago. Yet this horse was useless without a two-pound metal bit. With such a bit, the versatility of these animals matches their enormous strength. In the same way, the control of the tongue commands the whole person.

Ships that are driven by rough winds and strong gales yield to the direction of the relatively small rudder. In verse 4, the emphasis rests on a small thing that decides great direction. James could not have imagined the size of modern ocean liners. Yet, even they are directed by comparatively small rudders. In the same way, the small muscle in the human mouth can change the direction of human history. Adolf Hitler recorded his Nazi philosophy in the book *Mein Kampf*. Someone has noted that for every word in that book, more than a hundred lives were lost in World War II. Words do change the direction of history.

"How great a forest is set ablaze by a small fire!" (3:5). James described the tongue's destructive capacity. In James's day, a tiny spark could set the desert scrub brush afire. In the same way, an unguarded word can cause a firestorm of damage. In February, 1983, a firestorm ravaged southwestern Australia. Winds built to gale force; and, within hours, flames raced along miles of coast. Within hours, a broad arc of rich farmland and a fragrant eucalyptus forest lay reduced to scorched earth. Seventy-five people died, and property damage totaled more than $2,500,000.[7] James compared the tongue's destructive power to such a fire. A single word can char a person's reputation for life.

A Wheel on Fire (3:6)

A vehicle with its wheels on fire spells trouble. James wrote that the tongue "keeps the wheels of our existence red-hot" (3:6,

NEB).[8] In verse 6, James expanded his emphasis on the tongue as a fire. He restated his identification of the tongue with fire: "the tongue is a fire." But he went beyond that to identify the fire's nature and source. He further described the tongue as the inward incarnation of the outward world of sin. Even more, the tongue can spill a stain that defiles the whole body.

The tongue's fire continually is "setting on fire the cycle of nature" (3:6). In other words, the tongue sets on fire the entire complex of all human existence in each of life's varied relationships. This may refer to the human race as a whole or to individual lives. The verb tense would indicate that the tongue habitually, perpetually causes such human firestorms. Some have understood this to be a reference to the wooden chariot wheel of Roman times. When the wooden wheel lost its lubrication, it chaffed against the wooden axle. The result was a fire that moved from the hub of the wheel along the spokes to the outer circumference. The wheel blazed from the center to the rim. The tongue holds a strategic place at the center of every individual's life. What the tongue inflames at the center ultimately can touch every relationship.

What possibly could be the source of such a flaming evil? James clearly stated that the tongue is "set on fire by hell." The combustion from the flames of Gehenna sets the tongue on fire. The fact that the word *Gehenna* occurs only in verse 6 outside the Gospels underscores the terrible source of the tongue's inflammatory capacity. Literally nothing else in creation so relates to the flames of hell itself.

Thank God, the tongue also may be set on fire from heaven. At Pentecost, cloven tongues of fire rested over every believer in the upper room. That Pentecostal fire animated the apostles' tongues so that they could bear flaming witness to the Lord Jesus Christ and His resurrection. Today, Christ can control each tongue if each individual will give Him that control.

The Tameless Tongue (3:7-8)

The human race has tamed some creatures from every division of the animal kingdom. People can control created creatures but cannot conquer their tongues. God gave the human race power to subdue or domesticate the animal world. The creation story clearly states that God gave human beings this authority (Gen.

1:26,28-30). James stressed that this authority was established in the past and continues into the present: "For every kind of beast and bird, of reptile and sea creature, can be tamed and has been tamed by humankind" (3:7). Obviously, James did not mean that every single beast has been subdued. He used the traditional biblical division for the four types of animal life (Deut. 4:17-18). People have shown their ability to overpower and subdue some creatures from each division.

People have tamed beasts and birds. That is nothing new. Trained birds still fascinate observers; but, even in New Testament times, men trained birds to talk. Octavian, who later would become the Emperor Augustus, returned to Rome after he defeated Mark Anthony. He was given a raven trained to say: "Hail Caesar, victorious leader."[9] People can control a bird's tongue and subdue it for their own purposes. Yet the human race never has been able to subdue its tongues.

People have tamed sea creatures. Do you remember Flipper? The famous porpoise starred in one of the most popular television series of the 1960's. He was fictional, but Tuffy was real. Tuffy served as a member of the United States Navy's program Sealab II, off the coast of San Diego during the summer of 1966. He carried the mail between the surface and the crew, 205 feet below. He transported tools and even served as a lifeguard when one of the crew pretended to be lost.[10] Humankind has tamed the apparently untamable creatures of the sea. Yet, people never have learned to subdue their tongues.

James came to a stark, absolute conclusion: "No human being can tame the tongue—a restless evil, full of deadly poison" (3:8). The men who can control great beasts cannot control the small tongue. It is "an evil incapable of being quieted" (Williams).[11] The word translated *restless* belonged only to James's vocabulary in the New Testament and suggested anything uncontrolled or unruly. He used it in reference to the instability of a "double-minded man" (1:8). In 3:8, he stated that such divided or wavering thinking led to unruly talking. He used the same expression to refer to the disorder which characterized a jealous, factious, divided church (3:16).

One might think that James gave a counsel of despair. Conceivably, one might argue that if the tongue is such a restless evil, why even try to tame it? Augustine, the great fourth-century Christian, provided the answer to such a complaint: " 'He does not say that no one can tame the tongue, but no one of men; so that when

69

it is tamed we confess that this is brought about by the pity, the help, the grace of God."[12]

James saved the most striking warning for the last. The tongue is "full of deadly poison" (3:8). His warning sounds peculiarly apt. Just as poison usually exercises its death-dealing through the mouth, so the tongue acts in the mouth. One does not wish to have physical poison in one's mouth. Also, one should wish not to have spiritual poison—thoughtless words—in one's mouth. Would you eat poison? In Japan, some persons do. A favorite delicacy of the well-to-do in Japan is the unusual meal of "fugu," a small poisonous globefish or puffer fish. The fish carries a deadly poison which contains toxin up to 275 times more potent than potassium cyanide. The chefs who prepare this strange dish go through rigorous testing supervised by the government. In spite of all precautions, Japan admits that as many as two hundred persons have died in the last ten years from eating fugu. Most readers never would consider serving fugu at the dinner table. Yet, many meals are spiced with poisonous gossip about neighbors, business associates, and church members. Those who never would place physical poison in their mouths may spew verbal poison out from their mouths.

Consider for a moment the awesome power that James granted to the tongue. The tongue acts as a fire, stain, beast, and deadly poison. Wise people prevent fires, remove stains, cage dangerous beasts, and hide deadly poisons. Wise believers do the same with their words. If they do not, they will discover themselves to be the ultimate contradiction.

The Unparalleled Contradiction (3:9-12)

Someone has said that a person contains something of an ape and something of an angel. Nowhere does this contradiction appear more sharply than in one's speech. According to Jewish tradition, "the servant of R. Simeon b. Gamaliel . . . [was] sent into the market to buy first good and then bad food, [and] brought back tongue in either case." According to Plutarch, an Egyptian king told one Pittacus to cut out the best and worst meat of a sacrificial animal. In both instances, Pittacus cut out the tongue.[13] Who could deny that the same tongue that takes the Lord's Supper on Sunday can contradict all Christ stands for on Monday?

James framed the incongruity with a characteristically concrete example: "With it we bless the Lord and Father, and with it we curse men, who are made in the likeness of God" (3:9). Blessing on Sunday and cursing on Monday are not new. Some use the tongue religiously one hour and profanely the next. The Jews customarily repeated the phrase, "Blessed be He," after every mention of the divine name. Indeed, devout Jews of every age and sex repeated a certain prayer three times a day. The prayer was called "The Eighteen Benedictions." Each benediction ended with the same repetition: "Blessed art Thou, O Lord." Up to fifty-four times per day, God would be blessed in this prayer. Evidently, early Christians carried over something of this practice in prayer. On the other hand, James discovered that the same believers were cursing people. He even may have had in mind the angry curse that was spoken in inner-church party strife. James did not hesitate to use the term *we*. Even the half brother of Christ and pastor of the Jerusalem church did not consider himself immune from this temptation.

Verse 9 stresses a strong motivation against cursing. When an individual is cursed, the image of God is cursed in that person. Even in their fallen state, people still retain that image, although the image is fractured and clouded. To curse any person is to curse God's image in that individual. This is equal to cursing God. Devout Jews would not step on the smallest piece of scrap paper on the street lest it have written on it God's name. How quickly many people today trample God's image in another person with curses! James cried out in anguish: "My brethren, this ought not to be so" (3:10). His expression indicated the fatal inconsistency in such speech. The emphasis rests on the contradiction that is involved.

In *Pilgrim's Progress*, John Bunyan wrote of Talkative: "He was a saint abroad and a devil at home."[14] How many Christians speak with perfect courtesy to strangers and snap at their own families? How many teach God's Word on Sunday morning and tell the filthiest of stories on Monday? Proverbs 18:21 asserts: "Death and life are in the power of the tongue."

The tongue's contradiction appears literally nowhere else in nature. James was accustomed to the wells that flowed from the steep cliffs along the Jordan rift and the deep gulch through which the river flows. From some of the wells came fresh, clear, sparkling artesian water. From others may have come brackish, salty, noxious, bitter water. However, one thing never occurred: A person did not find fresh and bitter water coming from the same opening in the earth. What cannot come from the same opening in the ground can come from the same opening of the human body—the mouth. From it may flow almost at the same time bitter words and sweet words.

James concluded with an agricultural metaphor: Fig trees do not produce olives. Grapevines do not produce figs. Like produces like. A heart filled with anger produces angry words. A life sweetened by love for Christ produces Christlike words. In apple orchards, for instance, growers take twigs and branches from superior trees and graft them into inferior trees. The new plant produces fruit with exactly the same characteristics of the parents. It is literally a chip off the old block. Fruit always shows a family resemblance. Likewise, the believer's words should reflect a family likeness. The Father's attitude should characterize His children's speech.

Words and Wisdom (3:13-18)

One might get the impression that James introduced a new, unrelated subject at this point. Actually, a person's words and wisdom have a direct relationship. The wisdom in the mind determines the kind of words in the mouth. James explained that divine wisdom always manifests its presence in practical Christian behavior (3:13). Certain identification marks always characterize worldly wisdom (3:14-16). In the same way, divine wisdom leaves its footprints in life (3:17-18). To consider what James wrote would be wise.

Practical Wisdom (3:13)

This section appeals for the reader's self-assessment: "Who is wise and understanding among you?" The word "wise" points to deep discernment of the underlying principles of life. The term "understanding" relates to the practical, daily application of great, general principles. Taken together, the two words are the equivalent of theoretical and practical wisdom. My paraphrase would be: *Who among you really has the big picture and knows how to get things done?* How can one identify divine wisdom when it is operating in such a context? James stated that such a man would be wise and perceptive. Rather than an abrasive, belligerent attitude, God's wisdom produces gentleness. Such a man's "good deeds are done in humility, which wisdom prompts" (Williams).

72

C. T. Sharp was the wisest man I have known. He was not an educated man. A semiretired rancher, he had been by turns a mortician, professional boxer, cattle-truck driver, and hotel pastry cook. He had served as a Baptist deacon. In his eighties, he had served for years as deacon chairman in a small, semirural Texas Baptist church. Yet due to a lake development project, the community of the church suddenly had exploded with newcomers. As the church grappled with more changes than it had seen in its century of existence, the wise old deacon demonstrated divine wisdom. In physical, financial, and fellowship decisions, he literally held the church together by his gentle wisdom. The primary mark of that wisdom was a humble gentleness when he spoke. Such men and women produce the aura of God's presence.

Worldly Wisdom (3:14-16)

The world operates by its own wisdom. This wisdom is evident wherever movers and shakers gather to shape world, national, and community policy. Unfortunately, worldly "wisdom" may spill over into the church. James gave a snapshot of worldly wisdom at work. See if you recognize its marks.

Worldly wisdom demonstrates "bitter jealousy." The phrase refers to an unholy zeal which refuses to be reconciled. Nothing open, conciliatory, or redemptive takes place. Added to that trait is "selfish ambition" which refers to a spirit of factious rivalry, a party spirit. Such an attitude delights in the malicious, petty triumphs of one side over another. That attitude characterized the church at Corinth. It divided the church into factions over three human preachers. A fourth faction disdained all human leadership and wanted to get back to Jesus (1 Cor. 1:12). James shamed such an attitude, especially in the church. Such a party spirit exulted in what ought to have been the church's shame. That attitude contradicted the kingdom law of love (2:8) and was "false to the truth" (3:14).

James stated that worldly wisdom "is earthly, unspiritual, devilish" (3:15). Such wisdom is terrestrial, not celestial. It may belong to the cutthroat tactics of some business and political situations, but not to God's people. It is animal, not spiritual. James's word translated "unspiritual" suggests the activity of brute beasts, not born-again believers. Indeed, it is demonic, not divine, for it raises the devil in the heart of the opposer and the opposed. Unleashed in the church or in the world, it produces chaos. It opens a Pandora's box of every evil thing. (See 3:16.)

73

The wisdom that the world values produces selfish ambition. A scene from Benito Mussolini's life reveals this kind of factious, destructive ambition. One of his biographers reported that as Mussolini paced his room, she asked him what was his greatest ambition in life. Mussolini replied: "'I am obsessed by one wild desire. It consumes my whole being. I want to make a mark on my era with my will. A mark like this . . .' With his fingernails he scratched a chair back from end to end. 'Like the claw of a lion!'"[15] In the world or in the church, such selfish ambition demands that everything bend to its will, or else. It is worldly wisdom that will destroy a family, a church, or a fellowship in order to assert its own will. Such wisdom roots in hell.

Divine Wisdom (3:17-18)

God's wisdom acts differently. A single word characterizes heavenly wisdom as "pure" (3:17). In motive, word, deed, and attitude, God's wisdom works in purity. It is unmixed, unlaced with anything false or tainted. Nothing about it indicates a hidden agenda. It always can stand the light of day.

James continued to describe divine wisdom by presenting aspects of its purity. Just as droplets of water break down white light into the colors of the rainbow, James broke down the purity of wisdom into many colors. One color is peace. Such wisdom delights in and promotes peace. A second color is courtesy. Divine wisdom delights in gentleness. Grace ought to make people gracious. A compliant color in divine wisdom is openness to "reason" which seeks reconciliation. These qualities of God's kind of wisdom never will change. Human wisdom changes with every generation. What is "in" now will be "out" in the 1990's. God's wisdom remains the same. It sows seeds that later bear the fruit of peace.

Lessons for Life from James 3:1-18

Decide to tame the tongue for a definite period of time.—Try twenty-four hours as a beginning place. Measure each word before it is spoken. Place a guard by the mouth. Ask: *Does this edify?* If it does not, do not say it. See what this does to your speech over that period of time.

Measure your response in tense situations.—Do you display wisdom that is worldly, or wisdom that is divine? How do you tend to act or react when trouble arises at the office, in the church, or in the social circle? Do you demonstrate peace-making, or do you foster more divisions?

Are you reconciled to everyone in your circle?—Does a grudge exist that has not been settled? God's wisdom leads to a reconciling spirit. Perhaps the wisest thing would be to write a letter to a friend or a relative from whom you have been alienated. Seek to be reconciled. That is the wisdom which God displayed on the cross.

1. John Blanchard, *Gathered Gold* (Bath, England: the Pitman Press, 1984), p. 299.

2. Charles R. Swindoll, *Growing Strong in the Seasons of Life* (Portland, Oregon: Multnomah Press, 1983), p. 21.

3. Arthur Carr, *James in the Cambridge Greek Testament for Schools and Colleges* (Cambridge: University Press, 1896), p. 40.

4. From *The Bible: A New Translation* by James A. R. Moffatt. Copyright © 1935 by Harper and Row, Publishers, Inc. Used by permission.

5. From the author's observation of a plaque at Calvin's church in Geneva.

6. From the *New American Standard Bible.* Copyright © The Lockman Foundation, 1960, 1962, 1963, 1968, 1971, 1972, 1973, 1975, 1977. Used by permission.

7. *National Geographic,* February, 1983, pp. 152-155, 171-176.

8. From *The New English Bible.* Copyright © The Delegates of the Oxford University Press and the Syndics of the Cambridge University Press, 1961, 1970. Reprinted by permission.

9. Peter Muller, "Preposterous Pets Have Always been Our Status Symbols," *Smithsonian,* September, 1980, p. 83.

10. Robert Leslie Conly, "Porpoises: Our Friends in the Sea," *National Geographic* (September, 1966), p. 398.

11. From *The New Testament, a Translation in the Language of the People* by Charles B. Williams. Copyright 1937 and 1966. Moody Press, Moody Bible Institute of Chicago. Used by permission. Subsequent quotations are marked Williams.

12. R. J. Knowling, *The Epistle of St. James* (London: Methuene Co., 1904), p. 78.

13. Sophie Laws, *A Commentary on The Epistle of James* (New York: Harper & Row Publishers, 1980), p. 155.

14. Ralph Kirby, *The Pilgrim's Progress in Pictures* (Chicago: Moody Press, n.d.), p. 33.

15. J. Wallis Hamilton, *Ride the Wild Horses* (Nashville: Abingdon Press, 1952), p. 33.

Personal Learning Activities

1. James stated that not many of his readers should become _____. (Choose the correct answer from the list.)

   (1) Pastors   (3) Deacons
   (2) Teachers   (4) Missionaries

2. What three illustrations did James use to make his point that the tongue has power out of proportion to its size? _____ , _____ , _____

3. According to Dr. Gregory, our use of the tongue displays an unparalleled _____ . (Select the proper response from the list.)
   (1) Blessing
   (2) Creativity
   (3) Contradiction
   (4) Positive witness

4. James advised his readers to seek a practical, worldly wisdom that would help them to get along in life. ____True ____False

Answers:

1. (2); 2. A bit, a rudder, and a brushfire; 3. (3); 4. False.

6
Friend of the World, Enemy of God
James 4:1-12

Russian novelist Leo Tolstoy wrote of a man who was dominated by the driving desire for self-gratification. To possess land was his highest pleasure. Someone promised him that he could own all of the land he could walk around between sunrise and sunset on a given day. He began at a leisurely pace. However, driven by his ambition, he began to accelerate. He drove himself, sprinting faster and faster. His body blazed with fever. He stripped off his shirt and abandoned his boots. As the sun set, he flung himself toward his destination. He reached the starting line as the final rays disappeared in the west. Exhausted, he died. The only land he got was a grave, 6 feet by 2 feet.[1]

Tolstoy's unforgettable story underlines the raging power of the drive for self-gratification. Men and women die for their pleasures. James wrote to churches that were being divided by pleasure-seeking members. Ideally, God's wisdom gives peace (3:13-18). Actually, the churches to which James wrote experienced chronic hostility and sharp confrontations (4:1-6). The section 4:1-12 betrays the most passionate and intense feelings of the entire letter. Driven by personal pleasures, church members divided the churches. This portion of James divides into four emphases: (1) The pursuit for self-gratification leads to disaster in the church (4:1-3). (2) Obsession with one's own pleasure betrays worldliness.

Such spiritual adultery places the pleasure-seeker in conflict with God (4:4-6). (3) Such worldliness calls for urgent, radical repentance. James gave ten sharp imperatives—biblical bombshells that demanded repentance (4:7-10). (4) In this whole process, persons must judge themselves, not one another. To judge one's brother usurps God's prerogative (4:11-12).

When Believers Battle (4:1-3)

"What causes wars, and what causes fightings among you? Is it not your passions that are at war in your members?" (4:1). Why do believers battle? James's words do not address international wars, although the cause of such wars is the same. James wrote Christian churches that were embattled and strife-torn. The word "wars" indicates chronic, long-lasting hostilities. The term "fightings" refers to sharp outbursts, skirmishes that reveal the long-standing wars. Phillips translated: "But what about the feuds and struggles that exist among you?"[2] Like lava smoldering under the earth for years, some believers burn with belligerence. Like a volcano erupting, such anger surfaces in hot explosions. What causes the slow burn and the white-flash of angry confrontation?

James blamed church conflict on "passions that are at war in . . . [believers'] members." In verse 1, three words in his remarkable statement demand explanation: "passions," "war," and "members." **Passions** translates the word from which the English word *hedonism* comes. Literally, James charged: *Hedonisms are at war in your members.* The Greek word usually carries overtones of evil or unworthy enjoyment. Yet James did not refer exclusively to the "playboy philosophy." His word included any kind of self-gratification. The lust for position, power, or prestige dominates some lives that are unmoved by sensual pleasures. The pleasure of "getting it done my way or else" has caused many skirmishes in local churches.

The battleground for the passions of James's readers rested in their "members." Some interpreters have understood this to indicate the various members of the church. Selfish gratification propelled various church members with competing agenda toward inevitable conflicts. Another interpretation is more likely. Usually, in the New Testament, the word *members* refers to the members of the human body, the person's various parts that give the individual drives, lusts, and compulsions. James probably used the word

in that way. He graphically depicted selfish individuals who were walking civil wars. Frustrated desires for every kind of personal pleasure erupted in the church's life. What seemed to be the problem and what actually was the problem in the church were two different things. Every discerning reader knows that many church conflicts about buildings and budgets are not actually about buildings and budgets at all. Often, church disagreements conceal a whole spectrum of personal and vocational frustrations.

Desires for self-gratification are "at war" in every believer. Peter exhorted his readers to "abstain from the passions of the flesh that wage war against your soul" (1 Pet. 2:11). An occupation army still encamps and campaigns within every believer. Pleasures habitually lay siege to the soul. Each Christian must recognize and respond to pleasures on the continuing march within. The battle will not end until physical death or until Christ's return. Even though over the years strongholds of pleasure will be defeated, newer and more subtle ones will take their place.

Many churches face destruction by factious rivalry. Each person's pleasure is most important to that individual. As a result, the unbelieving world knows many Baptist churches more for heated business sessions than for Christlike concern in the community. Church members can—and do—inflict destruction with words.

Murder in the Aisles? (4:2)

Had things gotten so bad that Christians were killing each other? "You desire and do not have; so you kill" (4:2). These words present one of the difficult challenges to understanding James. Did James address the church or the world in verse 2? Did he mean that Christians literally murdered one another, or did he write figuratively? To understand that James made an observation about life in the world to the churches to which he wrote is best. The *Didache*, an early church manual, warned Chrisitans about murder: "'Be not angry, for anger leadeth to murder, nor jealous, nor contentious, nor wrathful, for of all these things murders are engendered'" (*Didache* 3.2.).[3] Even for Christians, conflicting pleasures can lead to violence. When one chooses pleasure instead of God, even murder can result. That James had in mind a particular church situation where Christians literally killed one another is unlikely. However, he did give the strongest possible warning about where conflict leads.

The calm prayer of personal petition presents the only alternative to church wars. "You . . . do not have, because you do not ask" (4:2). Christians battle with one another for pleasures they do not need. The only way out is for them to return to believing that *God* gives what the Christians really need. Confident expectation that God alone can meet the needs of any situation creates a calm sense of secure brotherhood, not an atmosphere of heated confrontation.

Right Things; Wrong Motive (4:3)

Self-centered believers pray, but they pray just like they live: "You ask and do not receive, because you ask wrongly, to spend it on your passions" (4:3). Church members may ask for the right things from the wrong motives. Already James had indicated that one may pray with the wrong attitude: doubt (1:6-8). In 4:3, James insisted that one may pray with the wrong objective: self-gratification. Earlier, he gave an example of the right objective for a believer's prayers: wisdom (1:5). God does not answer when one intends to squander the answer on personal lusts, selfish desires, or the mere acquisition of material gain. Such evil motivation in praying results in no action from God.

U. S. News reported the remarkable story of a forty-two-year-old man worth 40 million dollars. He lives in a 3-million-dollar mansion, drives a $90,000 Ferrari, a Jaguar, and a 44-foot speedboat. Seven years ago, he was hanging sheetrock and eating peanut butter sandwiches for lunch. Now, he owns three high-tech component companies.[4] Many readers' reaction would be: Why does God not do that for me? What would you do with it if God did? Today, some varieties of evangelical life in America reveal a shallow health-and-wealth philosophy. Some ministers teach that God wants to give people anything they dare to claim, regardless of motivation. God's eternal Word should correct such a distortion: "And this is the confidence which we have in him, that if we ask anything according to his will he hears us" (1 John 5:14).

Adultery Against a Jealous God (4:4-6)

"You adulteresses" (4:4, NASB)![5] James reached an emotional peak with this outcry. Unfortunately, the Revised Standard Version weakens James's thought by translating the words as "unfaithful creatures." The Greek word that James used clearly refers to adultery. Did James mean that church members regularly broke the Seventh Commandment? Likely, James referred to spiritual adultery.

The concept that God's people commit spiritual adultery through faithlessness to Him resounds in the Old Testament. Jeremiah cried out to Israel: "Only acknowledge your guilt, that you rebelled against the Lord your God and scattered your favors among strangers under every green tree" (3:13). The prophet compared God's people to an adulteress who gave herself randomly under Palestine's hilltop groves where Baal was worshiped. Hosea compared the adulterous behavior of the prophet's wife to Israel's spiritual adultery against Jehovah. Jesus used this imagery when He called the Jews an "adulterous . . . generation" (Mark 8:38). In the New Testament, the church becomes the bride of Christ (2 Cor. 11:2; Eph. 5:25-27). The lax church or the sinning saint commits spiritual adultery against Christ.

The image of adultery against God or Christ preserves a unique truth. When a married person commits adultery, he or she betrays a sweet, intimate, trusting relationship. In the biblical sense, the ultimate way a man or woman "knows" a mate is through sexual intercourse. To "know" someone else in the same way is to commit the ultimate betrayal of loyalty, trust, and intimacy. The adulterer does not break the law as much as he or she breaks the heart. Faithless believers break God's law. But more than that, they break God's heart.

Mutually Exclusive Friends (4:4)

The believer who courts the world's friendship takes a stand as God's enemy. Such spiritual adultery results in enmity against God. In James's sense, "the world" does not mean the world of nature. Nor does "the world" indicate the human beings whom God loves and for whom He gave His son (John 3:16). In James's sense, "the world" indicates the organized life of mankind that denies God's claim. Human institutions, activities, cultures, and pastimes organize themselves without reference to God's will. Today, one might call it "the spirit of the age." It represents the whole mixture of role models, heroes, slogans, obsessions, and fads that make up the contemporary scene minus God's will. It expresses itself in glossy magazine ads, alluring store windows, bumper stickers, tee-shirt inscriptions, and television situation comedies. The world is energized, living, breathing, grasping, and lusting for life—minus God!

Believers must love the world of people. They should love the world of nature. But they must not love the world in the sense of life organized without God. Christians must not court that world's heroes or make that world's goals their goals. They must not wed themselves to an order that has in it the seeds of its own death. The word translated "friendship" in verse 4 (elsewhere translated *love*) indicates affection for something; one form of the root word means *a kiss*. Believers must not kiss this godless age!

Nothing betrays people's affection for the world like the way they spend their money. The average American gives less than one dollar per year to foreign missions. Who could conclude anything other than a love for this world, not a love for God's kingdom?

Divine Jealousy (4:5)

Jealousy is not always bad. Gordon Clanton, a sociologist who long has studied the subject, explained: "'Jealousy is protection for love, a reaction to a perceived threat to a valued relationship.'"[6] Indeed, jealousy can be ugly when it is born of insecurity or possessiveness. On the other hand, jealousy can be a healthy response when a legitimate love relationship is threatened. Something is wrong when a husband or wife watches a mate be captured by another person without jealousy. Likewise, something would be wrong with God's love if He watched the world seduce His people without divine jealousy.

"Or do you suppose it is in vain that the Scripture says, 'He yearns jealously over the spirit which he has made to dwell in us'" (4:5)? No specific Old Testament Scripture makes the exact statement James quoted. He seems to have summarized a great deal of Old Testament thought about Jehovah as a jealous God. The Third Person of the Triune God indwells every believer. He does not intend to share living quarters with competing affections. He feels divine jealousy when believers give their affection to the world.

Greater Divine Grace (4:6)

A person might be tempted to despair. The pull of the world exerts itself ceaselessly and in increasingly subtle ways. Who is equal to James's demand? The believer is not left alone: God "gives more grace" (4:6). The believer's ability to overcome the world roots itself exclusively in God's grace. How does one appropriate that enabling grace to subdue worldliness? A person does so only by prostrating life before God in dependent humility. "'God opposes the proud, but gives grace to the humble'" (4:6; Prov. 3:34).

83

James's language indicates that God always places Himself in full divine battle array against every form of human pride. He intends to confront and defeat human pride in every form it takes. World-loving humanity experiences nothing but God's constant, loving counterattack. He will not let persons be satisfied with anything short of Himself. His stubborn love confronts people's pride.

The Bible contains striking stories of God's ability to reduce proud people to humble believers. Nebuchadnezzar presents the most arresting example of God's opposition to human pride. The Babylonian emperor crowed from the balcony of his palace: "'Is not this great Babylon, which I have built by my mighty power as a royal residence and for the glory of my majesty?'" (Dan. 4:30). These words no sooner leaped from his lips than God sent him to the pasture to live and eat like an ox! Literally, he moved from the palace to the pasture. Today, psychologists call this malady lycanthropy, the belief that one is an animal. Nebuchadnezzar's specifc form of sickness was boanthropy, the belief one is an ox. He remained in that condition until he "'learned that the Most High rules the kingdom of men and gives it to whom he will'" (Dan. 4:32). God knows how to humble the highest person. No individual will live and die in arrogance before God. The God who moved an emperor from the throne of the world's seventh wonder to the back forty of Babylon can deal with anyone's pride just as decisively today.

Eight Steps Toward Christian Repentance (4:7-9)

Back-sliding believers can come back to a renewed relationship with God. He offers a heavenly homecoming to every sinning saint who returns. W. T. Conner insisted that the deepest repentance of the Christian life comes *after* conversion.[7] Like peeling away layers of onion skin, the sensitive believer finds more and more for which to repent. As believers go farther out to the world in witnessing, they also explore deeper layers of repentance.

James gave eight clearly stated steps to repentance. He stated these steps by ten imperative verbs that leave no doubt about the nature of returning to God:

1. Submission—"Submit yourselves therefore to God" (4:7). This command covers all of the steps like an umbrella. It enfolds the following nine commandments which unfold this imperative.

The tense of the verb indicates a decisive, urgent, clearly focused act. The word **submit** simply means *to place or arrange one thing under another, to subject or subordinate one person to another*. In verse 7, it indicates the *voluntary willingness to align oneself under the authority of another*. God sets Himself against the proud; therefore, set yourself under God.

The world-famous founder of the Salvation Army, General William Booth, stated that many others were more intelligent than he, better preachers than he, more qualified than he. His secret: "'God has had all there was of me.'"[8] More than anything else, God needs people who will submit themselves to Him. Education, qualifications, or high position without submission mean nothing to God. Is every arena of your life arranged under God's will: home, business, social life, monetary policy, physical discipline, and personal influence? The first step to Christian repentance is examining and submitting life to God.

2. Resistance—"Resist the devil and he will flee from you" (4:7). Earlier, James stressed personal responsibility in temptation (1:13). In 4:7, he clearly indicated supernatural activity in temptation. Boldly, abruptly, and decisively the Christian should oppose Satan. In exactly the same way God opposes pride in full battle array, the believer must oppose Satan. Elsewhere the believer is told to "withstand" Satan (Eph. 6:13) and "resist him" (1 Pet. 5:9).

Satan takes dead aim at every believer. Four confrontations with Satan in the Old Testament show the range of his targets. He targeted Eve's mind (Gen. 3:1-7), Job's body (Job 2), David's will (1 Chron. 21), and the high priest Joshua's conscience (Zech. 3). With God's inspired Word, imparted grace, indwelling Spirit, and interceding Son, the believer actively must resist Satan.

Denial discourages the devil! When Jesus resisted him, "the devil left him, and behold, angels came and ministered to him" (Matt. 4:11). Not only did Satan flee, but God gave special grace to the One who resisted. Jesus could have used His divine power to thwart Satan. Instead, He chose to use the weapon available to every child of God: the divine Word. Jesus provided the example of reading and memorizing the Word. He did not have a concordance in the wilderness!

C. S. Lewis delighted the ages with his *Screwtape Letters*. In that book, the brilliant British Christian created the correspondence between an apprentice devil assigned to a new, young Christian and the apprentice's experienced devil-uncle. Lewis wrote the book to spite the devil. He quoted as a motivation the words from Sir Thomas More: "The devil . . . the prowde spirite . . . cannot endure to be mocked."[9] When one resists and mocks the devil, he flees. Try it!

3 Return—"Draw near to God and he will draw near to you" (4:8). This categorical promise stresses the mutual, reciprocal nature of a person's approach to God and God's approach to that person. When one takes a step toward God, God already has taken a step toward that individual. The psalmist emphasized the same truth: "The Lord is near to all who call upon him, to all who call upon him in truth" (Ps. 145:18). God always responds like the father of the prodigal: "While he was yet at a distance, his father saw him and had compassion, and ran and embraced him and kissed him" (Luke 15:20). Many sinning saints refuse to let God act in His goodness. They say to themselves: I've gone too far this time; He never could forgive what I have done. Such hopeless despair never comes from God. Rather, it results from Satan's accusing activity. God's Word calls Satan "the accuser of our brethren . . . who accuses them day and night before our God" (Rev. 12:10).

Warren Wiersbe made a clear, critical distinction between God's activity and Satan's: "When the Spirit of God convicts you, he uses the word of God in love and seeks to bring you back into fellowship with your Father. When Satan accuses you, he uses your own sins in a hateful way, and he seeks to make you feel helpless and hopeless."[10]

Resist Satan and draw near to God. Both are effective, and both are necessary.

4. Cleanse—"Cleanse your hands, you sinners" (4:8). Outwardly, repentance involves spiritual cleansing of the instruments of sin, which are designated as the "hands." The hands stand for the person's entire outward life. James addressed those who habitually missed the mark. Often, their hands participated in aimless sinning. Such outward sin must experience a *catharsis*, to use James's word, a thorough cleansing in the blood of Christ.

The Old Testament priests had to wash their hands in a bronze laver filled with water, "lest they die" (Ex. 30:20). This was elementary education for God's family. As the material water removed physical filth from their hands, they became aware that spiritual filth also had to be removed. The Jews had a custom of praying with uplifted hands (Pss. 28:2; 134:2). The hands that a person folds in prayer or lifts up to God must be clean hands.

5. Purify—"Purify your hearts, you men of double mind" (4:8). Mere outward cleansing never suffices. Inward purity alone

pleases God. In verse 8, James picked up his favorite expression for the divided Christian, double-minded. Earlier, James warned that the wavering, divided believer cannot experience victory in answered prayer (1:6-8). He demanded that the double-minded saint repent. In order to purify, one must unify. Soren Kierkegaard entitled his famous book *Purity of Heart Is to Will One Thing*. He could have taken his title from James.

The psalmist suggested outward and inward cleansing:

> Who shall ascend the hill of the Lord?
> And who shall stand in his holy place?
> He who has clean hands and a pure heart (Ps. 24:3-4a).

Neither clean hands nor a pure heart occurs alone, for clean hands receive their life's blood from a pure heart.

6. Feel—"Be wretched" (4:9). None of James's advice sounds as strange to the contemporary, compromising Christian as this. James demanded that Christians feel their sorrow deeply when they realize their spiritual condition. James called for an experience of grief when the worldly Christians recognized how far away they had gone. Persons have to acknowledge who they are before they can disown who they are. Paul had to acknowledge that he was a "wretched man" before he could shout with joy, "Thanks be to God through Jesus Christ our Lord!" (Rom. 7:24-25).

Wretchedness is not a room where God wants one to live. It is a door through which one must pass on the way to renewed fellowship. God wants believers to feel miserable guilt only as long as it takes them to repent. James spoke with startling intensity in order to shake worldly believers.

7. Respond—"Mourn and weep" (4:9). The inner sense of wretchedness usually displays itself in an outer, emotional response. "Mourn and weep" reflects a deep grief that cannot be concealed in its intensity. Some people who should cry, do not. Confronted with the wretchedness of sin, they refuse to respond with any emotion. Surely, James did not refer to a phony show or superficial display of emotion. However, believers who are faced with the fact of sin should respond with the deepest feeling.

8. Reverse—"Let your laughter be turned to mourning and your joy to dejection" (4:9). Penitent believers display a marked contrast from their previous behavior. Loud, raucous, pleasure-loving laughter turns to quiet, sober introspection. The word translated "laughter" in the Old Testament referred to a feast of fools who

had declared their independence from God. The joy repentance forsakes is the joy of a profane life that has no tension with the world. When the enormity of sin crashes into a life, a reversal from the superficial gaiety and noisy levity of contemporary life takes place. The downcast, heavy heart of the penitent publican illustrates the contrast (Luke 18:13).

Certainly James did not mean that laughter is sinful. He did not mean that repentant believers never should laugh again. James would agree with the psalmist who wrote that after God's people repented, "Then our mouth was filled with laughter, and our tongue with shouts of joy" (Ps. 126:2).

The steps to repentance conclude just as they began, with a call to humility: "Humble yourselves before the the Lord and he will exalt you" (4:10). Even in the most extreme cases, humble repentance can change lives.

Judging the Judges (4:11-12)

Is not judging and criticizing others always easier than to judge oneself and to repent? Evidently the unrepentant, worldly Christians whom James addressed found far more to criticize in their brothers than in themselves.

James addressed his words to the "brethren." Within the Christian community, some believers habitually disparaged other believers. "Speak evil" reflects the backbiting, faultfinding, harsh criticism that too often has characterized Christian people. Reading the newspaper, the contemporary world sometimes must think of Christians: Behold, how they hate one another! Peter taught Christians that when the truth about a brother is harmful, one should cover it in love rather than repeat it in criticism (1 Pet. 4:8).

James gave two compelling reasons to refrain from harshness toward other believers. First, to disparage a brother disparages God's law. The Royal Law insists that believers love one another (2:8). To slander a brother attacks the King of laws. Such harsh criticism gives a declaration of independence from God's reign and rule. Harsh critics commit mutiny in God's kingdom. They revolt against God's sovereignty. They declare: God's law is good for others, but it is unnecessary and invalid for us. They shatter God's law as surely as Moses broke the tablets at Sinai. Few believers understand the radical seriousness of judging and disparaging brothers and sisters.

What is more, to slander a brother usurps God's place. God is the only Lawgiver and Judge. He alone has the right to enforce His edicts with life or death (4:12). The arrogant, critical Christian tells God: "Move over. Your throne has room for me, too!" This attitude means that harshly disparaging a brother is tantamount to blaspheming God.

Consider people's powerlessness and puniness compared with God: "Who are you that you judge your neighbor?" (v. 12). How can finite, sinful individuals dare to judge someone who is like themselves? If you sense such an attitude in yourself, bow before God in the eight steps of repentance.

Lessons for Life from James 4:1-12

Each reader should assess his or her role in the inevitable friction and conflict in church life.—Do I always initiate and contribute to the strife? Do I ever seek to make peace? How often does the criticism at church reflect unresolved conflict in my life that simply explodes in the church?

How do my values, heroes, and life-style differ from my neighbors who do not claim Christ?—Do I have a different attitude toward the world than my non-Christian co-workers?

Growing Christians continually repent.—Is your attitude one of self-examination and deliberate repentance? Or, is your life filled with loud, noisy activity that masks your need for quiet, spiritual reflection?

---

1. See J. Wallace Hamilton, *Ride the Wild Horses* (Westwood, N.J.: Fleming H. Revell, 1952), p. 54.

2. Reprinted with permission of Macmillan Publishing Co., Inc. from J. B. Phillips: *The New Testament in Modern English*, Revised Edition. © J. B. Phillips 1958, 1960, 1972.

3. R. J. Knowling, *The Epistle of St. James* (London: Methuen & Co., 1904), pp. 95-96.

4. *U. S. News & World Report*, 3 Oct. 1983, p. 63.

5. From the *New American Standard Bible*. Copyright © The Lockman Foundation, 1960, 1962, 1963, 1968, 1971, 1972, 1973, 1975, 1977. Used by permission.

6. Morton Hunt, "How Jealous Are You?" *Readers Digest* (Oct. 1983), p. 27.

7. See W. T. Conner, *The Gospel of Redemption* (Nashville: Broadman Press, 1945), p. 199.

8. Paul Lee Tan, *Encyclopedia of 7,700 Illustrations: Signs of the Times* (Rockville, Maryland: Assurance Pub., 1979), p. 1367.

9. *The Screwtape Letters* (Time Incorporated, NY: C. S. Lewis, 1961) p. xxv.

10. Warren W. Wiersbe, *The Strategy of Satan* (Wheaton, Ill.: Tyndale House, 1979), p. 85.

Personal Learning Activities

1. According to James, the "passions that are at war" in Christians' members cause _____ and _____. (Choose the correct answers from the list.)
   (1) Diseases   (3) Wars   (5) Dishonesty
   (2) Crimes   (4) Immorality   (6) Fightings

2. To stress his readers' unfaithfulness to God, James used the image or metaphor of (select the proper response from the list):
   ____(1) Rebellion.   ____(3) Revolt.
   ____(2) Adultery.   ____(4) Indifference.

3. According to Dr. Gregory, in 4:7-9 James gave eight steps toward _____. (Choose the proper answer from the list.)
   (1) Success   (3) Maturity
   (2) Happiness   (4) Repentance

4. What two reasons did James give for Christians to refrain from harshness toward other believers?

Answers:

1. (3),(6); 2. (2); 3. (4); 4. To disparage a brother disparages God's law; to slander a brother usurps God's place.

7
Presumption and Perversion
James 4:13 to 5:6

A song that was popular boasted, "I did it my way." James confronted the greedy, affluent business community with withering denunciation. The previous section condemned Christians' love of the world (4:4). That love demonstrated itself in the affluent people's sins. James targeted two groups: merchants (4:13-17) and landlords (5:1-6). Presumption, arrogance, and exploitation marked their lives.

Mistaken Merchants (4:13-17)

Mercenary merchants mistook their plans for God's plans. They thought that they could play God with their own futures. People's desire to control the future shows the futility of such arrogant planning. No one on earth ever tried to control his future as the Egyptian pharaohs tried to control theirs. Each one exploited thousands of people for dozens of years to assure his future. Their efforts failed.

The earliest pharaohs tried to ensure their futures by having their bodies buried in above-the-ground pyramids like those at Giza near Cairo. Within decades, grave robbers looted the tombs and stole the mummies. Then, later pharaohs moved their tombs three hundred and fifty miles up the Nile to Luxor (ancient Thebes). There, in a remote area that resembles a moonscape, the pharaohs carved their tombs out from the solid stones under the ground. The pharaohs literally started planning their tombs at the time of their coronation. Yet despite the remote site, the strict secrecy, and diversionary shafts, the tombs were plundered soon after they were sealed. The lust for gold and hatred for enemies spoiled the pharaohs' plans. Out of more than sixty tombs in the Valley of the Tombs of the Kings at Luxor, only one tomb remained almost untouched—that of Tutankhamon, "King Tut." History teaches a striking lesson from those plundered tombs: Those who worked the hardest to secure their futures without God lost the most. God's Word teaches the same truth.

Perilous Planning (4:13)

A group of merchants eagerly riveted their attention to a map of the Roman Empire. In the electric atmosphere of anticipation, they planned when and where they would go, how long they would stay, and how much money they would make. A confident attitude of materialistic certainty filled the room. Did James consider that unethical? No, he did not consider making business plans unethical. He stated that making plans without acknowledging God's sovereignty was illogical and unspiritual. It was illogical because one did not even know what the next day would hold (4:14). It was unspiritual because it did not reckon with God's will (4:15).

The background of James 4:13 reflects the Jewish genius for business. That genius developed during the Babylonian captivity. Documents discovered in Babylon reveal the intensive Jewish commercial transactions there. The Jews' language after the captivity, Aramaic, became the language of trade. The Mishna, a collection of Jewish precepts, contains extensive advice on personal conduct by Jewish traveling businessmen. It reveals that the Jews were involved in international traffic in silk, satin, vases of gold, mirrors, and even slaves. The word "trade" (v. 13) reflected the ambitious, traveling wholesaler rather than the local retailer. James 4:13 pictures a group of Jews or Jewish Christians who were ambitious businessmen with big plans for the future.

In every way, the businessmen demonstrated a worldly presumption about the future. They presumed about time: "today or tomorrow." This attitude suggested that opportunity for future business rested in their power. They presumed about mobility: "We will go." No human can say for certain whether he or she will

92

be able to move a single body part tomorrow. No one ever slams a car door or walks down an airplane's loading ramp with any certainty of destination. They presumed about location: "such and such a town." The English translation does not catch the significance of the Greek idiom. In Greek, the expression suggests definite plans about were they would go. They had a cock-sure attitude about their destination in business travel. They presumed about their durability: "spend a year there." In arrogance, they acted as if they could assure their longevity.

Most of all, the businessmen made an arrogant presumption about their success: "trade and get gain." Here, the merchants betrayed the mainspring that wound up their lives and made them tick. Everything grounded itself in personal, material gain. James arranged the verbs in 4:13 to end in this climax. The hidden agenda behind all of the businessmen's proud presumption about the future was personal gain.

James did not mean that sound business planning is sinful. He certainly did not mean that business travel never should be planned. He did indicate that every plan for the future should be submitted to God's sovereignty. The psalmist wrote: "Commit your way to the Lord; trust in him, and he will act" (Ps. 37:5). A simple, practical plan commends itself for such submission of the future to the Lord. Take time every morning to consider the day's agenda before God. Take an hour at the end of every week to submit the coming week's agenda to the Lord. Take a day every month to reflect on your life's goals and their relationship to God's will. These planned checkpoints will enable you to keep the tentative nature of your future clearly in focus.

What people plan and what happens often contrast strikingly. In 1923, an important planning meeting took place at the Edgewater Beach Hotel in Chicago. "Attending this meeting were nine of the worlds most successful financiers. Those present were: the president of the largest independent steel company; the president of the largest utility company; the president of the largest gas company; the greatest wheat speculator; the president of the New York Stock Exchange; a member of the President's cabinet; the greatest 'bear' in wall street; head of the world's greatest monopoly; president of the Bank of International Settlements."[1]

An investigator determined the destiny of the nine men twenty-five years later. The president of the steel company lived on borrowed money the last five years of his life and died bankrupt. "The president of the greatest utility company . . . died a fugitive from justice and penniless in a foreign land. The president of the largest gas company . . . was insane. The greatest wheat speculator . . . died abroad, insolvent. The president of the New York Stock Exchange . . . was . . . released from Sing Sing Penitentiary. The member of the President's cabinet . . . was pardoned from prison so he could die at home. The greatest 'bear' in Wall Street . . . died a suicide. The head of the greatest monopoly . . . died a suicide. The president of the Bank of International Settlements . . . died a suicide."[2] Even though they planned the future for personal gain, the future they planned did not happen.

Future Frailty (4:14)

Those who make plans for future years cannot be certain about tomorrow: "whereas you do not know about tomorrow" (4:14). Jesus told the parable of the big fool with little barns. He, too, was certain that he had many years to build and to gather. In a single night, his soul was required of him (Luke 12:16-21). He worried about little barns and thought that he had big amounts of time. Instead of concern about bigger barns, he should have pondered the possibility of less time to live. In every generation, people trip over the trap of what is really big and what is really little.

The correct perspective recognizes the finitude and frailty of human life: "What is your life? For you are a mist that appears for a little time and then vanishes" (4:14). Literally, James's language suggests that human life is a phenomenon for a little while and suddenly is no longer a phenomenon. The Bible uses a variety of metaphors to express the brevity of life: a declining shadow (Ps. 102:11), a whiff of breath (Job 7:7), a vanishing cloud (Job 7:9), and a wild flower (Ps. 103:15). Robert Burns, whose tragic life underscored his poems, wrote poignantly of life's brief pleasure:

> But pleasures are like poppies spread:
> You seize the flow'r, its bloom is shed;
> Or like the snowfalls in the river,
> A moment white—then melts for ever.[3]

The shocking bevity of life's influence surprised me several years ago as I stood in Westminster Abbey near the Houses of Parliament in London. In that extraordinary building, many of the greatest men in western civilization are buried. I stood before the statues of Benjamin Disraeli and William Gladstone, the two greatest prime ministers in nineteenth-century England. At the height of the British Empire's widest extension, these men's names were on everyone's lips. Two imposing statues tower over their tombs. As I listened to two American tourists, they said: "Disraeli! Gladstone? Hmm. I wonder who they were? Some old poets, I guess."

Because of my background in European history, I was amused by their missing the mark. However, amusement turned to sadness as I pondered how two great men could be forgotten in the next century. I had the same experience when I asked a London cab driver, "Take me to the Metropolitan Tabernacle, the church of Charles H. Spurgeon." The cabbie never had heard of either. The man alleged to be one of the greatest preachers since Paul was not remembered in the city where he preached. The brevity of life and its influence are remarkable. Unless God remembers us, we are undone.

Careful Contingency (4:15)

In light of life's brevity, what should the Christian's attitude be about future planning? One might react with terrorized fear. Another might respond with paralyzed inaction. Hedonism says: "Eat, drink, and be merry, for tomorrow we die." Nihilism says: "Life means nothing." Existentialism says: "Life has no essence; you cannot plan it." What is the Christian attitude toward the uncertain future?

The Christian attitude is submission. The Christian submits to God's will: " 'If the Lord wills, we shall live and we shall do this or that' " (4:15). The Christian inscribes over all of his or her plans: "if the Lord wills." This raises the question of whether the sincere believer actually should state this phrase before any future plans.

The phrase "if the Lord wills" can become a mere formality that is devoid of any meaning. One may hear repeatedly in the Moslem world the Arabic statement, inshallah, which simply means, "if God wills." However, in some instances it has become a tricky way of avoiding future responsibility. Obviously, the phrase can be trivialized if it is attached lightly to everyday activities. For example, one should not say: "We will go buy a hamburger for lunch, God willing," or "I will shoot par on the back nine, God willing." Such talk trivializes the phrase and runs dangerously close to taking God's name in vain, which means without sufficient weight. That Paul did not always use these words when he spoke of his future plans is interesting. Sometimes he did, and sometimes he did not (1 Cor. 4:19; 16:5-7; Rom. 15:28).

To live life with the attitude, without verbalizing the words, is far more important than to use the phrase without the underpinning attitude. However, as a whole, Christians should use the phrase far more than they do.

A Warning (4:16-17)

"You get a certain pride in yourself in planning your future with such confidence" (4:16, Phillips).[4] Nothing can breed arrogance like a humanistic certainty of continued health, prosperity, and life. John called this "the pride of life" (1 John 2:16). It is the arrogance of self-sufficient living without dependence on God. The omission of stated dependence on God is not an inconsequential thing: "Whoever knows what is right to do and fails to do it, for him it is sin" (Jas. 4:17). These words may relate only to the immediate context. Christians who omit to plan their futures with God in mind commit sin. On the other hand, the words may relate to all that has gone before. In a real sense, these words form a summary of the entire Letter of James. What one omits to do may be as serious a sin as what one does.

Reprimanded Rich (5:1-6)

Arrogant pride about future plans may lead to a more dangerous possibility. Those who plan and plot for future gain can become unjust, unscrupulous, and unfair toward others. They can use people to fill their own greed. They can manipulate the weak to feed their egos. James unleashed a tirade against the selfish, godless rich. Nothing in the Bible exceeds its vehemence against those who live for material prosperity alone. Some contemporary popular "health and wealth" theology casually joins Christianity with a voracious materialism. Under the slogan "name it and claim it," this superficial materialism promises Christians anything they may want. From James 5:1-6, one can guess James's attitude toward such perversion of Christian values.

Brace Yourselves! (5:1)

The godless rich receive only an ominous warning. Before an airliner makes a crash landing, the passengers are told to brace themselves for the inevitable impact. In 5:1, James did the same for the insensitive materialists: "Brace yourselves; judgment is coming." The "rich" whom James addressed appear to have been non-Christians. Unlike the people who were addressed in 4:1-10, verse 1 has no call to repentance, no hope of salvation.

"Come now, you rich . . . ." implies that getting the attention of the godless affluent was not easy. Nature is replete with examples of animals that appear to be alert and aware, but who, in reality, are lost in slumber. The horse actually can sleep while standing up. The huge hippopotamus snoozes in the water. Bats nap while hanging upside down, suspended from their feet. More remarkably, the rich person who forgets God may appear alert, aware, successful, and on top of things; yet, in reality, that individual is unaware of judgment's impending doom.

"Rich" translates a Greek word that, combined with another Greek term, comes into English as *plutocrats*. **Ploutos** means wealth and **krateia** means rule or power. Hence the word in Greek and English denotes the people who are ruled by the god of wealth. The godless rich in James's world accumulated wealth in several ways. James had in mind exploitive landlords who abused poor peasant farmers. Others charged high interest that crippled the poor.

James called on the rich to "weep." Scholars agree that this is not a call for repentance. Rather, James warned them of coming disaster and called for anguish as the only proper response for the judgment that no one could stop.

For James, God's certain judgment on godless materialists was so inevitable they should begin weeping before judgment. This grief should express itself in a "howl for the miseries" that were coming on them (v. 1). Twenty-one times in the Old Testament, the word *howl* describes the violent grief of those who stood face-to-face with divine judgment. In horror of the coming disasters, the godless rich were to weep in anticipation. The vivid use of the present tense *coming* suggests that the waves of successive judgments could be seen on the horizon. Like tidal waves, nothing could stop them. The rich people's only appropriate response was to weep and mourn with heart-rending wretchedness and intensity.

For Christians in the "me-generation" of the 1980's to forget Jesus' sobering words is easy:

'But woe to you that are rich, for you have received your consolation. Woe to you that are full now, for you shall hunger. Woe to you that laugh now, for you shall mourn and weep. Woe to you, when all men speak well of you, for so their fathers did to the false prophets' (Luke 6:24-26).

Today, the values of Americans are distorted with greed. Recently, the highest paid corporate executive in America received $22,823,000 for his annual salary. The average pay for baseball players is more than $300,000 per year.[5] Scarcely more than a decade ago, their average pay was a fraction of that figure. On a typical Sunday afternoon, a professional golfer can make thousands of dollars for the best score on seventy-two holes of golf. Some of these people are professing Christians. Whether or not any one of them deserves such wealth is not the point. The point is that in such an environment, luxuries quickly become necessities. James warned against a personal and national value system that catered to such a philosophy.

Long ago, Amos pronounced God's judgment on people who lived in animalistic self-gratification while they ignored the needy around them. Amos' words have a strange, contemporary ring. He warned those who reclined on expensive beds, ate delicate gourmet foods, listened to idle music, drank fine wine in greater quantities, and anointed themselves with expensive perfumes and after-shave lotions (Amos 6:4-6). His words almost describe an indulgent American society.

W. A. Criswell, pastor of First Baptist, Dallas, since 1944, identifies affluence as the single greatest threat to Southern Baptists. It will bless or curse the denomination, depending on the response of God's people to stewardship.

Rotted Riches (5:2-3)

James's readers accumulated riches in three basic forms: hoards of food, accumulation of garments, and collections of precious metals. From the standpoint of God's judgment, each already had been blighted, had rotted, and had tarnished. James was so certain of God's judgment on godless wealth that he used the perfect tense verbs of future judgment. Judgment was so sure that James viewed it as already having taken place.

James could see mildew rotting the people's excesses of food, moths gorging themselves on expensive garments, and precious metals tarnishing. Although gold does not rust, Strabo, the Greek geographer, added an interesting comment on James's world. Strabo noted a vapor arose from the Dead Sea that caused brass, silver, and even gold to rust. He probably referred to a change of color in the metals due to the strong vapors from the Dead Sea. Even so, as the wealthy man looked in horror at the dimming luster of his treasure chest, he should have considered his wealth's temporal and vanishing quality.

James echoed Jesus: "'Do not lay up for yourselves treasures on earth, where moth and rust consume and where thieves break in and steal, but lay up for yourselves treasures in heaven, where neither moth nor rust consumes and where thieves do not break in and steal'" (Matt. 6:19-20).

How dramatically life can cause money to lose its luster! Robert Hastings recalled the experience of American soldiers evacuating Corregidor during World War II. As they left the famous rock in the Philippines, everything that might have been of value to the enemy had to be destroyed, "including neatly stacked bundles of U.S. currency. The tired, battle-weary soldiers watched quietly. One soldier picked up a hundred dollar bill and used it to light a cigarette, saying, 'I always wanted to do this.' Time was running out on Corregidor, and money had very little meaning" in the face of the coming enemy. Paul Geren's *Burma Diary* detailed a similar situation: Refugees streamed from Burma to India during the early days of World War II. Survival was their only concern. "Finding their money of no value, many of them threw it away." They realized that in order to escape, a given weight of food would do more to save their lives than the same weight of gold. As such, their precious riches rotted![6]

Modern American goldbugs might do well to ponder the refugees' story. If the threatened calamity actually comes, how will they turn gold into food? If an ounce of gold suddenly is worth $6,000, who will make change for a loaf of bread? Any ultimate security short of God never is adequate.

Indeed, godless wealth will act as testifier and tormentor in the judgment to come. James warned: "Their rust will be evidence against you and will eat your flesh like fire" (5:3). Their rotted riches would become Exhibit A at God's final trial. Unused garments that could have clothed the naked will scream out accusation. Grain that might have filled empty stomachs, but had been stored until it mildewed, will take the witness stand. Both will testify that they were hoarded in selfishness rather than shared in generosity.

Then in some strange way, the testifiers will become the tormentors for eternity. The rust that destroys what it clings to will become the fire of God's judgment. James exhorted the materialists to look at the tarnish which stained their silver and to see in it the fire of judgment that would more than tarnish them. The perishing quality of their riches should have revealed the perishing quality of their lives in God's judgment. Indeed, those who treasure up wealth may be treasuring up nothing but judgment.

Americans especially never seem to lose the delusion that great money is great happiness. Gail Sheehy was almost poor, if not poor. She lived with her baby in a fourth-floor-walkup apartment on East Seventh Street in Manhattan. Quietly, she wrote her book *Passages*, which became a huge best-seller. Did sudden wealth solve her problems? No. " 'It makes me sweat a lot more, it makes me embarrassed and guilty—I mean, truly, it's terrible.' " When it became clear that *Passages* would make her a lot of money, Sheehy chatted with her Random House editor. His advice sounded prophetic: " 'Yes, well. Money. You will find, Gail dear, that it will now be a dull ache in the back of your head. *Forever*.' "[7]

" 'It was so ominous,' Gail says, 'and it was exactly how I felt!' "[8] Few who pursue wealth consider that it will be a dull ache in the back of their heads. The consistent testimony of many affluent people would be just that. Yet, James warned of something even more ominous. Wealth that is used without God can become not a dull ache but a burning fire forever. The pervasive, temporal satisfaction with wealth is only a harbinger of things to come in the judgment.

Money Talks! (5:4)

When rich persons get their way because of money, we often say: "Money talks." James also said "money talks," but in a different way. Money gained or withheld unjustly will talk at God's judgment. In fact, such tainted money taken fraudulently from innocent people cries out to God at this moment. Furthermore, God hears and responds in judgment. This represents James's first specific charge against the unjust rich.

Earlier, James's warnings of judgment were general; in verse 4, he made a specific charge. Day laborers mowed and harvested the fields for absentee landlords. Such modestly paid laborers were numerous in first-century Palestine. Their earnings were pathetic, and survival could be a serious matter if they found no daily work. To work under the blistering sun only to find no pay at the end of the day was even worse. James described such humble, powerless, poor men bilked of their meager wages by powerful men who owned large estates. The word *fields* suggests huge estates, extensive lands. James's word suggested that, initially, the meager wages were withheld and continued to be withheld.

James dramatically depicted the withheld wages' shrieking cry.

100

The cry was as though the starving, unpaid workers were too weak to cry; therefore, the withheld wages cried out! From inside the cheating rich man's securely locked treasuries, the money cried out. Money does talk; it can even cry out to God. Withheld money cries out against wrong and robbery; it cries for vengeance and deliverance.

The God of the Bible makes clear the affluent people's responsibility to the poor in all matters. Jesus stated: "'The laborer deserves his wages'" (Luke 10:7). God gave the same instruction to His people during the Exodus: "'The wages of a hired servant shall not remain with you all night until the morning'" (Lev. 19:13). The end of the day was the time for just pay. In many instances, to deprive a laborer could leave him and his family on the edge of starvation. This was so important that Moses included the same emphasis in his farewell address. Indeed, Moses expanded and strengthened the emphasis: "'You shall not oppress a hired servant who is poor and needy, . . . you shall give him his hire on the day he earns it, before the sun goes down (for he is poor, and sets his heart upon it); lest he cry against you to the Lord, and it be sin in you'" (Deut. 24:14-15).

The God of the Bible is not locked in the sanctuary. He is present in humanity's marketplace. He watches every transaction between traders. He sees the poor and the plutocrats who plunder them. In fact, James asserted: "The cries of the harvesters have reached the ears of the Lord of hosts" (5:4). Here, James employed an expression used 246 times in the prophets, who also were concerned about injustice. *Lord of Sabaoth,* Lord Omnipotent, God Almighty, or "Lord of Hosts" all translate the same Hebrew words. The expression pictures God as the Commander of heaven's armies. He leads innumerable, invisible spiritual hosts. The word even has cosmic dimensions. He commands all the twinkling, starry hosts. He is the God of the Exodus and the Conquest, Gabriel and Michael, planets and stars. Yet the cosmic God's ears stay turned to the defrauded poor persons' cries. The unjust rich will meet that God in judgment. They may brace themselves, but they will be no match for Him. The tables will be turned. Those who exploited the powerless will find themselves confronted with ultimate power. Justice will be more than served. What an awesome day that judgment will reveal!

Stop the Banquet (5:5-6)
In contrast to the deprived poor people, the unjust rich persons

lived life as a perpetual banquet. The past-tense verbs look back on the indulgent, affluent people's lives as a whole. In verses 5-6, James wrote as though he were looking over a just God's shoulder at the judgment and listening to His verdict. Such a reflection well might sober anyone.

The rich lived "in luxury." The phrase suggests a life of delicacy that moved in the orbit of a soft, effeminate, lax existence that broke down discipline. This was the rich man's style of life in Jesus' famous parable (Luke 16:19-31). President Theodore Roosevelt advocated what he liked to call "the strenuous life," a combination of mental and physical discipline. The turn-of-the-century population was amazed that the rough rider could read a book a day and preside over the nation. The unjust rich lived lives dedicated to weakening pleasures that were just the opposite of anything strenuous. James's word "pleasure" suggests a life of prodigal waste, wanton hedonism, or satisfaction of physical appetites. While the defrauded, hungry poor waited outside the ornate gates, the luxuriating rich people feasted and played inside.

The rich liked to slaughter choice veal for gourmet meals. James ironically turned that phrase another way: "You have fattened your hearts in a day of slaughter" (5:5). While they gorged themselves on choice cuts of freshly slaughtered beef, they were fattening themselves for the slaughter!

The phrase "day of slaughter" probably refers to the great final day of retribution when God will judge His enemies. In the apocalyptic language of Revelation, the same imagery describes God's final judging activities (Rev. 19:17-18). Those who lived animalistic lives like brute beasts whose only concern was the next mouthful would meet God. Those who lived to slaughter veal for the next banquet would find themselves facing a similar, sudden end one day.

God would confront the hedonistic rich with the evidence that they used the legal system to bilk the righteous, poor people. "You have condemned, you have killed the righteous man" suggests more than murder (5:6). Those words were used for judicial murder. The sinful rich abused and slanted the judicial system to silence the defrauded poor. If the defrauded persons dared to complain, they found that the place of justice had been bought and paid for by those who had defrauded the poor. A plaintive quality echoes from the words "he does not resist you" (v. 6). A poor, faithful follower of Jesus did not attempt to resist evil (Matt. 5:39). Even if the poor man did, he could not have matched the power of the rich people who owned the system of justice. Take courage! The Lord of Hosts will be the equalizer. The meek will inherit the earth (Matt. 5:5). The perverse value system of the Christless world will be turned upside down. Mary sang of this even before the Holy Child's birth. She foresaw that Christ's reign would reverse all lost people's fallen values:

> He has put down the mighty from their thrones,
> and exalted those of low degree;
> he has filled the hungry with good things,
> and the rich he has sent empty away.—(Luke 1:52-53)

Lessons for Life from James 4:13 to 5:6

Christians need to plan for the future, but they must do so with faith and submission to God's will rather than with presumption.—Faith is the opposite of presumption. Faith commits the present and the future to a loving Father; it never takes tomorrow for granted.

Believers must have a healthy realization that life is fragile and brief.—Such a perspective reminds us that life is a gift and each day is to be used fully for God.

Christ's followers must guard against a pride or an arrogance that produces a false certainty concerning health, prosperity, and even life itself.—The opposite of such unhealthy pride is a humility that submits one's way to God.

Christians need to develop and maintain the proper view of money.—How money is earned, how it is used, and the place it occupies in one's life are crucial. A person can be consumed with the desire to amass wealth, can employ unethical means to get it, can use it or hoard it selfishly, and can let it become a god. Or, one can work hard and honestly to earn money, can share it with those who are in need, and can use it to further God's redemptive purpose.

Godless materialism will face God's sure judgment.—Things are deceptive gods that cannot sustain life. They last for a time and then pass away. To live for this brief, temporal life alone is to forfeit continuing life with God.

The Scriptures consistently confirm God's attentiveness to the poor and the defrauded.—People cannot run roughshod over the powerless and helpless persons without facing the inevitable consequences of such wrong.

———
1. B. J. Chitwood, *A Faith That Works* (Nashville: Broadman Press, 1969), p. 104.
2. Ibid., p. 105.
3. *The Complete Works of Robert Burns*, "Tam O'Shanter" (New York: Houghton Mifflin Co., 1897), p. 91.
4. Reprinted with permission of Macmillan Publishing Co., Inc. from J. B. Phillips: *The New Testament in Modern English*, Revised Edition. © J. B. Phillips 1958, 1960, 1972.
5. *Parade Magazine*, June 16, 1985, pp. 4-7.
6. Robert J. Hastings, *My Money and God* (Nashville: Broadman Press, 1961), p. 33.
7. Andrew Tobias, *The Only Investment Guide You'll Ever Need* (New York: Bantam Books, 1983), p. 144.
8. Ibid.

Personal Learning Activities

1. In 4:13, James warned against _____.
   (Choose the correct answer from the list.)
   (1) Materialism   (3) Unethical acts
   (2) Worldly presumption   (4) Planning for the future
2. According to Dr. Gregory, the Christian attitude toward future planning is _____. (Select the proper response from the list.)
   (1) Self-assertion   (3) Deliberate neglect
   (2) Refusal to plan   (4) Submission
3. James called on the godless rich to repent. ____True ____False
4. According to James, God hears the cries of the _____
   _____. (Select the proper answer from the list.)
   (1) Penitent   (3) Righteous
   (2) Sick   (4) Defrauded poor

Answers:

1. (2); 2. (4); 3. False; 4. (4).

8
Until Then: Living Until the Lord Comes

James 5:7-20

Runners would confess that the most grueling race is the 400 meter run. Longer races are run, but the 400 meter is the longest sprint. No runner can sprint indefinitely. As runners reach 390 meters, their hearts pound and their lungs feel as if they will explode. Were the runners not sure that the 401st meter promises rest, they could not endure.

James 5:4,6 describe the tribulations that materially poor believers faced in the race of faith. Crushed by the unrighteous rich, they could not resist. Yet, James assured them that they would not have to sprint forever. God would intervene, but they had to learn how to live until the Lord comes. James gave three basic exhortations on how to live until then.

Believers must live with long-suffering, steadfast endurance (5:7-12). Christians should live with appropriate, effective prayer in all circumstances (5:13-18). Christ's followers should spend the time until Jesus comes rescuing those who lose patience and wander from the way (5:19-20).

Until Then: Live with Patience (5:7-12)

A single expression casts its shadow over the remainder of James's letter: "be patient." The conjunction "therefore" looks back to the trials that the poor believers experienced at the hands of the unjust rich (5:1-6). In essence, James wrote: *In this age, believers can do little about their enemies. Do not resist, much less avenge yourselves. Therefore, develop the spiritual discipline of patience. Let that virtue ripen until the Lord comes. Don't get even; get patient.*

The English word *patient* weakly translates James's original word. "Long-tempered" would be a better translation. English has the corresponding phrase "short-tempered." James combined the Greek word **makro** (long) with the word **thumia** (anger). **Makrothumia** means to be long-tempered. It reflects self-restraint that does not retaliate easily or quickly. With people, it means never to lose patience or hope. With events, it means never to admit defeat. The term could be defined as long, careful thought before one acts or responds emotionally.

Makrothumia contains another shade of meaning. It indicates someone who has the power to crush by retaliation but refuses to do so. How often do we tell ourselves: I've got him where I want him now? For people to be long-tempered indicates a refusal to retaliate, even when it would be easy. Sometimes, little puppies play around an old hound. They may nip his ears or scratch his nose. With one swipe of his paw or snap of his teeth, he could kill or maim the pups, but he does not. He has the power to retaliate, but he refuses to use it.

Repeatedly, the Bible attributes the attitude of long-suffering to God in His relationship to persons (Ex. 34:6; Neh. 9:17). When people act with patience toward others, they only are imitating God's attitude toward them. The patient attitude is a fruit of the Spirit (Gal. 5:22). It is the uniform of the Christian life that one should put on daily (Col. 3:12).

No one can sprint forever. James set a limit to endurance: "until the coming of the Lord." The phrase indicates Jesus' second coming. James used the word that Jesus used three times in Matthew 24 to describe His return. The word indicated a ruler's state visit. Our King is coming! That is the reason for patience now and the reward of patience then. Not even Christianity tells one to be long-suffering forever. An end is in sight when faith will be vindicated.

Patience is a Christian virtue. James gave three concrete examples to help us until then.

The Patient Farmer: Wait for the Harvest (5:7b-9)

"Behold, the farmer" (v. 7b). James called on his readers to ponder and reflect on the life of the Palestinian peasant farmer. The small farmer planted scarce seed and hoped for the best. During the last weeks before harvest, his whole family could suffer hunger. Year by year, the family's entire life depended on the harvest. A bad year could result in the loss of the land, hunger, or death. In patience, he recognized that the harvest was "the precious fruit of the earth" (v. 7b). That phrase suggests that the whole process rested outside his power. After he had planted the seed, nothing he could do hastened the harvest. As he watched with affection, emotion, and constant expectancy, he only could be patient.

The whole process led to nothing unless the crop received "the early and the late rain" (v. 7b). That phrase magnified the human helplessness and the farmer's absolute patience. In Palestine, the early rain started in October or November. It softened the brick-hard soil that had baked under the relentless sun. Unless that rain came, the farmer could not plow; and the seed would not germinate. The latter rain that matured and ripened the crop fell in March and April. Unless that rain came, the crop would be stunted or nonexistent. Expanded Jewish law contained regulations for prayer about the two rainfalls.

Imagine the careworn face of the Hebrew farmer whose concerned gaze moved from the bone-dry soil to the faces of his hungry children. Only patient prayer to God could provide hope.

The 1980's might be called the *Now* generation. We want physical fitness, financial success, and peer group approval *now*. Many people demand happy homes, fulfilling careers, and rewarding leisure time *immediately*. Yet, on every hand, signs point out that this attitude toward life is not working. Drug abuse and stress-related illnesses indicate that life without patient waiting on God does not work. Recently, a cardiologist entitled his book *Is It Worth Dying For?* He argued that "hot reactors" respond to every frustrating situation with angry stress which constricts their coronary arteries. He counseled people to be "cool reactors," which is only another way to say, "Be patient."[1] Twentieth-century medicine demonstrates the practicality of first-century Christianity.

In contrast to the life of patience, James prohibited an attitude of irritation: "Do not grumble, brethren, against one another" (v. 9). Constant pressure of oppression from the outside can cause believers to murmur against those closest to them—fellow Christians. The word *grumble* suggests a moan, groan, complaint, or suppressed feeling of ill will. Bickering and fault-finding undermine the community that waits for the Lord's coming. James warned against believers' mutual recrimination against one another. Such carping, criticizing Christians should realize that "the Judge is standing at the doors" (5:9). That refers to the certainty, suddenness, and nearness of the Lord's return.

The day will come when an angelic messenger will cry, "All arise." The Judge of the universe will enter His judgment hall. How ashamed will be Christians who are caught indulging in petty criticism! Many Christians do not grasp how seriously God takes their grumbling criticism against other Christians. Patient living demands a radical refusal to complain about other believers. In fact, Christians are to pray for one another instead of grumbling against one another. When believers actually pray for other Christians, they seldom criticize their brothers and sisters in Christ.

Prescription for Patience: Consider the Prophets (5:10)

James advised: "Take the prophets" (5:10). They present striking examples of patience under long-term hardships. "Suffering" emphasized the *passive* nature of their misfortunes. Like great rocks by the sea, they simply had to take the pounding of waves of opposition. "Patience" highlights the *active* quality of persistent, godly living in the face of tribulation. Suffering did not come because of sin in their lives but because they "spoke in the name of the Lord." James established a parallel between the prophets and Christian leaders. Both are on God's side against evil.

James's word *example* repays careful study. It literally referred to beautifully formed letters in a copy book. Students used such books with tracing paper to learn how to form correct letters. James challenged his readers to trace their lives over the prophets' lives.

Jeremiah's life presents an arresting example of such persistent patience. God called him as a teenager who was living in a tiny village. After Jeremiah preached his first message of radical repentance, his own family tried to kill him. What a way to start in the ministry! Undaunted, the young preacher stood in the gate of the Temple on a great feast day. He told the assembled people that their worship was worthless because they had no intention of obeying God (Jer. 7). The religious establishment tried to kill him after his first public sermon (Jer. 26:11). The religious leaders beat him and stretched his limbs painfully in stocks (Jer. 20). After he wrote his prophetic book, a godless king cut it into pieces and burned it (Jer. 36). Finally, all of this got to Jeremiah. In a fit of depression, he blamed God and lamented his birth (Jer. 20:7-18). Yet, God would not allow Jeremiah to resign.

Through all that happened to him, Jeremiah endured. Decade after decade, the lonely, single prophet cried out God's Word. At the end of his life, the Jewish refugees carried him to Egypt with them. They could not live with him, and they could not live without him. Obedient living stretched Jeremiah to the breaking point, but he endured hardship.

How pale contemporary Christian complaints look alongside Jeremiah's life! One quits a Sunday School class because of a personal slight. Another quits giving because he does not like the color of new carpet in the sanctuary. Another stops attending worship because the pastor preaches five minutes past noon and infringes on the football game on television. How pathetically shallow such excuses look compared to Jeremiah's life! Baptists often stress the gospel of a good start. We also need to emphasize equally the gospel of a good finish. What Paul told Timothy remains true today: "Share in suffering as a good soldier of Christ Jesus" (2 Tim. 2:3).

American Christians would do well to reflect on modern-day Jeremiahs who live with steadfast endurance. Some Russian Baptists have endured harrassment, intimidation, persecution, torture, and death for their faith. Do you suppose that they missed church on Sunday night because their favorite television program was on? Do you think they missed prayer meeting because of a spring shower? Today, Southern Baptists could learn from those who are paying an awesome price for their faith.

The Superbowl of Endurance: Job (5:11)

If steadfast endurance had an Olympics, Job would win the gold medal. Job made his only New Testament appearance in the book of James. Just as James used Abraham as the great example of faith, he used Job as the highest example of endurance. Whereas people attacked Jeremiah, circumstances attacked Job. Job lost his health, his wealth, and his family. Even his wife told him to commit suicide (Job 2:9). His friends accused him of some terrible, hidden sin. Even God seemed to be silent through thirty-seven chapters of the book.

Yet, James insisted: "You have seen the purpose of the Lord" (v. 11). At the end, God revealed His purpose. The text has a play on words. The Greek word *telos* can mean both "end" and

109

"purpose." One translator rendered this phrase: "You have seen how the Lord treated him in the end" (5:11, NEB).[2] You cannot understand the purpose until you come to the end. In the surprising conclusion, God restored Job's friends, family, and fortune. Job lived another hundred and forty years and saw four generations of his family (Job 42:10-17). Just when Job thought life was over, it all really began. At the end of Job's trials, God appeared; then, all of Job's life became different. James wanted every believer to know that at the end of the Christian's trials, Christ will appear.

Job learned two things about God that he would not have known apart from his endurance. "The Lord is compassionate and merciful" (5:11). The word for compassion could be rendered "bigheartedness." Job learned God's heart while enduring trial. At the end, he also knew God's mercy.

In the midst of trying circumstances, James warned Christians not to swear but rather to tell the simple truth (5:12). When the heat is on and days are difficult, for some people swearing replaces praying. In trying circumstances, Christians should use simple, true, transparent speech. The Lord will not hold the person guiltless who takes His name in vain (Ex. 20:7). We live in a society that seems to find telling a lie far easier when the heat is on. The only hope for integrity in business or in government is those who obey James's words: "Let your yes be yes and your no be no, that you may not fall under condemnation" (5:12).

Spiritual Endurance in a Physical Generation

The patient farmer, the persistent prophets, and the patriarch Job—all argue simply but eloquently for the value of spiritual endurance. Today, many in our generation place overwhelming value on physical endurance. Consider the Ironman Triathalon World Championships. This race of 2.4 miles swimming in the ocean, 112 miles of biking, and 26.2 miles of running is held in Hawaii. The world record is nine hours, five minutes, and fifty-seven seconds. If one survives the start of the race, which consists of hundreds of swimmers jockeying for position, in spite of being kicked and trampled by fellow-swimmers, the participants only have to look forward to a grueling 112-mile bicycle ride. That famous ride extends along the Kona Coast and offers no mercy. The course slices through the 180-year-old lava flows. The bleakness defies description. But when that is finished, a marathon race awaits the participants. Network television transmits this race to millions. The winner is hailed as a triumphant example of endurance.[3]

Does our generation ever place a similar value on spiritual endurance? Physical feats prove the body's ability to endure and to win a perishing prize. "Every athlete exercises self-control in all things. They do it to receive a perishable wreath, but we an imperishable" (1 Cor. 9:25). Contemporary churches desperately need an "Ironman Triathalon" of spiritual endurance. The age cries for men and women who possess a whatever-it-takes kind of faith. The hour calls for a Christian commitment that endures regardless of physical inconveniences, social ostracisms, financial sacrifices, or vocational jeopardies. "When through fiery trials thy pathway shall lie, My grace, all-sufficient, shall be thy supply: The flame shall not hurt thee: I only design Thy dross to consume, and thy gold to refine."[4] Ringing sermons or flaming deeds are not the final requirement. Endure, and you will know God's reward.

Until Then: Live with Praise and Prayer (5:13)

In every circumstance of life, the believer relates first to God. In bad days, one prays. In good days, one praises God. In days of illness, one calls the church to prayer. In two earlier sections, James dealt with prayer. The object of a believer's prayer should be for wisdom to face life's testing times (1:5-8). One's motive for prayer never should be one's own passions; it should be for God's will to be done. In verses 13-18, James summarized and expanded his earlier teaching on prayer.

In Bad Days, Pray (5:13a)

In 5:13, James referred to misfortunes other than illness, which he addressed at length. The word "suffering" particularly emphasizes the internal distress caused by outward circumstances. James may have had in mind the persecution just described. Rich landowners had bilked from the poor believers their just wages. James certainly intended to contrast the difference between swearing (5:12) and praying in life's difficult days. How many people greet difficulty with a curse, an oath, or an obscenity?

Christians should turn to God in prayer (5:13). Believers should not grumble, seek to retaliate against those who do wrong to them, or even simply "grin and bear it" like a Stoic. Rather, Christians should turn to God for relief and deliverance. Testimony of the power of prayer in difficult days fills the Psalms:

> "Call upon me in the day of trouble;
> I will deliver you, and you shall glorify
> me" (Ps. 50:15).
> When he calls to me, I will answer him;
> I will be with him in trouble,
> I will rescue him and honor him (Ps. 91:15).

In Good Days, Praise (5:13b)

The Christians' earliest recorded impressions on pagans highlighted the believers' joyful praise. Pliny, the governor of Roman Bithynia, wrote to Emperor Trajan in AD 111. His letter is regarded widely as the earliest outside reference to believers by a Roman ruler. Pliny wrote: " 'They are in the habit of meeting on a certain fixed day before it is light, when they sing in alternate verses a hymn to Christ as God.' "[5]

How should believers react when they are "cheerful" (5:13b)? We often turn to God in life's dark, difficult days. Many turn to God less often in life's bright, prosperous days. To walk with a full cup is more difficult than with a half-empty cup. James urged the believers to turn to God in praise when everything was going well, as much as they turned to Him in prayer when things were going badly.

The word translated "praise" first referred to plucking an instrument such as David's harp. James may have had in mind singing David's psalms, but more than that was involved. James's word indicated both public and private expressions of praise (1 Cor. 14:15; Eph. 5:19; Col. 3:16). Such praise to God actually intensified the joy of positive experiences.

Have you ever noticed your first impulse when something gives you great joy? It is the desire to praise it to another person. The act of praising the thing intensifies and enlarges your own pleasure in it. When you sit mute, your enjoyment of a good thing diminishes. By the same principle, when you ascribe praise to God for any experience, you enrich, round out, and intensify that experience.

The great reformer, Martin Luther, stressed the positive power of praise in music: " 'The devil is a sad spirit and makes folks sad, hence he cannot bear cheerfulness; and therefore gets as far off from music as possible, and never stays where men are singing, especially spiritual songs.' "⁶ The Lord inhabits the praise of His people.

Special Prayer for the Sick (5:14-18)

No section of James touches on the raw edge of human need as does the section on prayer for the sick. Because of that, it deserves detailed treatment. An understanding of this passage can bring great joy. To misunderstand it may bring unnecessary heartache to the ill and their families. In 5:13-14, James wrote to the suffering, the cheerful, and the sick. The advice to the third group—the sick—differs considerably from the advice he gave to the first two groups.

In the first two instances, prayer and praise did not necessarily involve anyone else. However, the sick man was to call on the church elders. Another significant change rests in the tenses of the verbs that describe the actions. The first two groups are to *keep praying* and *keep on praising* as a normal habit of daily life. However, in the case of the sick the verb tense indicates an immediate action to be done on only one type of occasion: sickness. The third significant difference is that James gave the sick persons more details than the former two groups. Those details demand a careful examination.

The Ill Christian (5:14-15*a*)

James asked if anyone among the readers were sick. He took for granted that believers would suffer illness. He used two words for illness in this passage. Both words specify the physical impact of illness rather than the nature of the illness. In verse 14, the word **astheneō** emphasizes any kind of weakness and is the most frequently used word for sickness in the New Testament. The English word *asthenic*, which means weak, came directly from the Greek verb. In verse 15, the verb form **kamno** stresses the weariness and fatigue that come from illness. In the biblical world, the word was used specifically but not exclusively for gout and diseases of the eye. Taken together, the two words stress the weakness and weariness that come to the sick person as a result of a disease.

Note that the two words for illness never refer to demon possession in the New Testament. The word in verse 14 always applies to physical disease when indicating illness. It never applies to demon possession. In three cases, the condition it describes is distinguished carefully from demon possession (Luke 4:40-41; 8:2; Acts 5:16). Nothing in this section addresses exorcism of demons that cause illness. In James 5 or elsewhere, the New Testament gives no support for some contemporary teaching that all illness relates to demonic activity.

The Call for the Elders (5:14)

James gave the sick man advice: "Let him call for the elders of the church." The sick person was to take a particular initiative. He was to call on a body of men (the noun is masculine, plural) from the church to come to him. This implies a serious illness. The implication is that calling for the elders should not be done lightly. Curtis Vaughan quotes Thomas Manton: " 'The elders must not be sent for upon every light occasion, as soon as the head or foot acheth, . . . but in such grievous diseases wherein there is danger and great pain.' "[7]

Who are the "elders of the church?" Southern Baptists generally do not recognize a separate group of church officials called "elders." James may be the earliest writer who mentioned elders in the New Testament. The elders are not mentioned in the Gospels, but they appear suddenly in Acts and in the Epistles. The word certainly refers to a definite church office in James 5:14, not merely to the older men in the church. Presumably one, many, or all of the elders might respond to the sick person's call. Also, the "church" is the local assembly of believers.

The office of elder probably was modeled after the Jewish synagogue. In a Jewish town, the custom was for the holiest rabbis to go to a sick neighbor's house in order to pray for him. That James's first Jewish Christian leaders would take some of their organization for the church from their own synagogue background seems obvious.

The passage implies that the elders were to go to the sick person as church representatives, not because their office carried a special healing function. Elsewhere, Paul wrote of a definite charismatic gift of healing. That gift was given to some believers by the solemn act of the Spirit, but it was not associated specifically with the church elders (1 Cor. 12:9,28,30). Interestingly, James did not ask the person to send for a faith healer. James told the person to send for a body of men from the local church.

Today, if a sick Southern Baptist wished to send for "the elders," who should be invited? Certainly, today "the elders" would include the ordained ministers of the gospel in the local church. I also would include the ordained deacons among those who may be called "elders." In the New Testament, the Greek words for elders, bishops (overseers), and pastors (shepherds) were used interchangeably for those with pastoral duties. (See Acts 20:17,28; Titus 1:5,7; 1 Pet. 5:1-2.) However, no biblical reason exists as to why both groups could not be included in a general call to the elders.

The Elders' Prayer (5:14)

When the elders assembled, James commanded: "Let them pray over him, anointing him with oil in the name of the Lord." Three elements comprised their prayer: the prayer itself, the anointing with oil, and the invocation of the name of the Lord (Jesus). Unfortunately, curiosity about the anointing with oil has overshadowed the dominant element: believing prayer. The major theme of this section is prayer. The word "prayer" or "pray" occurs in every verse (5:13-18).

James specifically designated the elders to pray "over" the sick person. This obviously describes a situation in which the sick person was bedfast and lying down. Origen of Alexandria, a third-century Christian commentator, understood James to mean: stretching their hands over him. James may have meant that, or stretching their hands toward him, or even placing their hands on him, although that is not mentioned. James could have meant simply standing over the person in bed.

Related to the prayer over the sick person was anointing him with oil. The verb tense would allow this anointing to take place *before* the prayer or *along* with the prayer, but not after. The passage does not specify where the oil should be placed. The oil specified is olive oil, for that is the specific Greek word used. No evidence exists that the oil was "consecrated" or "holy" oil. Mark 6:13 states that Jesus' disciples "anointed with oil many that were sick and healed them." According to the Gospels, Jesus never commanded or practiced anointing with oil. Scholars debate whether the oil was medicinal, symbolic of prayer, or an actual vehicle for God's power.

In the ancient world, both Jews and Gentiles used oil for healing. The Jews were permitted to prepare such a solution even on the sabbath. The Old Testament refers to oil's healing qualities (Isa. 1:6). In the biblical world, oil could soothe and cleanse wounds (Luke 10:34). Josephus related that Herod the Great's chilled, aching body was warmed in oil. Other ancient sources recommended oil for toning the muscles, seasickness, paralysis, and toothache. According to this view, one might translate James 5:14b: Giving him his medicine in the name of the Lord. The verb translated "anointing" that James used never appears in the Gospels as anointing for religious or spiritual purposes. It always referred to anointing for cosmetic or medicinal purposes. Thus, some respected scholars have viewed the oil as totally medicinal. They understand that James joined together "taking your medicine" with prayer.

That James referred exclusively to a "medical" use of oil apart from "spiritual" symbolism is unlikely. Such a distinction would have been foreign to the wholistic understanding of healing in 5:13-15. W. A. Criswell noted: "One thing that is certain is the psychological implication. It is good to do something to help people believe they can be well."[8] When Jesus healed the blind man, He made clay out of the spittle. No one would say that the clay alone had a medicinal effect. It was a helping symbol of God's healing power in Christ. The warm, soothing oil was a visible sign of the power of prayer.

Should Baptist believers anoint a sick person with oil when such a person calls for the elders? John Wilkinson observed that "Jesus did not command or advise it."[9] James attributed the healing power to God through prayer, not through oil. Some respected believers understand that the use of oil does not form an essential part of the church's healing ministry. Because of the potential for misunderstanding or for abuse, the use of oil by Baptists should call for cautious consideration. Certainly oil should not be used lightly, indiscriminately, or casually. For example, James 5:13-15 offers no basis for the use of oil in public services or indiscriminately by a pastor in hospitals. If a group of Baptist deacons (or elders) use oil, it only should be in the exact circumstances that James outlined. The sick person should call them to his bed; they should pray over him in the name of Jesus; and quietly, they should use a modest amount of oil. Perhaps the decision to use oil or not to use it should be left to the sick person who calls the leaders. If the ill individual feels the need for such anointing, let it be done. If he does not, remember that the use of oil is permitted but not commanded. Above everything else, that no power resides in the oil must be made clear. All power belongs to God; that power is appropriated through believing prayer.

The Healing Act of God (5:15)

The elders pray a "prayer of faith." The prayer that may result in healing must be prayed in trust in and commitment to God. James 1:5-8 requires that every prayer be offered in that attitude if it results in God's action. As the result of such praying, James stated that God may do three things.

First, "The prayer of faith will save the sick man" (v. 15). This raises an interesting question of interpretation. The Greek word for *save* and *heal* is the same. Did James mean that such praying would save the man from sin eternally in the spiritual sense of salvation? The New Testament never states that one person may be saved by another's prayer. It often refers to one being healed physically by another's prayer. In James 5:15, the promises refer to the individual's physical healing. He will be made whole physically by believing prayer.

Next, James promised that "the Lord will raise him up." Once again, an interesting problem of interpretation appears. The Greek word translated "raise" is the usual word for Jesus' resurrection. However, it also refers to the physical standing up of someone who has been sick. For instance, when Jesus healed the lame man, the man arose and took his pallet to walk away (Mark 2:9-12). In James 5:15, the word **raise** means, *He puts him on his feet again with new strength and vitality.*

Finally, the healing has a spiritual dimension: "if he has committed sins, he will be forgiven." The Jewish rabbis taught that a direct connection existed between sickness and sin. One said: "No sick person is cured of his disease until all sins are forgiven."[10] In contrast to this view, Jesus stated that a direct correspondence between sickness and sin does not exist in every instance (John 9:2-3). Yet in other instances, Jesus seemed to identify a relationship between sickness and sin (Mark 2:5; John 5:14). Paul insisted that the sins of some sick and deceased Corinthian believers had caused their illnesses and deaths. Their sin related to abuse of the Lord's Supper (1 Cor. 11:30). In the Old Testament, David stated that his sin had caused him physical illness (Ps. 32).

James 5:15 suggests that sin may be the cause of illness, but not necessarily. As Sophie Laws carefully stated: "James thinks of a possible, but not inevitable, association rather than a direct cause and effect relationship."[11] James chose a word which implies that a relationship between sin and the believer's illness might exist. *If* the brother has sinned, as part of the total act of healing his sins will be forgiven. Verse 15 reflects the Christian understanding of good health and wholeness. Our generation virtually idolizes physical fitness. Yet no one is truly fit unless the whole person has been healed, physically and spiritually.

James 5:15 presents a difficulty because of the unqualified nature of James's promises. Without any qualification, he stated that God would heal the person. Yet the prayers of thousands of godly people have not been answered positively in the matter of healing. Many commentators agree that such praying must be subject to God's will. "If God so wills it" must be implied in all such praying.

The healings that Christ performed while He was on earth had a special significance. "Besides being works of mercy, they were signs of his messianic identity. . . . Supernatural healings in equal abundance to those worked in the days of Jesus' flesh may not be his will today. The question concerns not his power but his purpose. We cannot guarantee that, because he was pleased to heal all the sick brought to him then, he will act in the same way now."[12] Paul was left with his "thorn in the flesh" (2 Cor. 12:7-9). He wrote the Philippian Christians concerning their messenger Epaphroditus and his illness. Even though Epaphroditus had brought the offering from Philippi to Paul in the Roman prison, he almost died (Phil. 2:25-30). Paul claimed no special power to heal him. Only by an act of God's mercy did Epaphroditus survive.

Often, human weakness deepens human dependence on Christ. The weaker we know ourselves to be, the more prone we are to lean on Christ. Many who have passed through times of illness would confess a new dimension to spiritual life after the sickness. Today, some individuals insist that healing is provided in Christ's atonement. Spiritual healing is provided, but perfect physical health is promised only in heaven.

The Prayer of a Righteous Man (5:16-18)

In the context of mutual confession, the prayer of a righteous man explodes with potency (5:16). The emphasis is on the righteousness of the one praying and the specific nature of his request. The word translated "great power" relates directly to the English word *energy.* Elijah is an example of such praying. In James's day, Elijah stood tallest among the Hebrew prophets. He was able to start and stop the rains of heaven when he prayed. Yet, he was a man of human frailties just like us. He was an eruptive man filled with human passions. On the one hand, he could stand boldly before the prophets of Baal. On the other hand, he would run away

from Jezebel in a fit of melancholy and depression. Yet, his praying moved God's might to change the elements. James suggested that such praying does not belong only to "super saints." Men and women with common frailties have moved the power of God.

Spiritual Restoration a Healing Opportunity for All (5:19-20)

Spiritual sickness results when a believer wanders from the truth. The word "wander" comes from the Greek word for *planet*. The ancients watched the skies and detected that the planets wandered among the fixed stars in the heavens. In 5:19, James referred to a believer who wandered in the midst of other believers who remained fixed in their devotion to Christ. Whoever turns such a brother from error "will save his soul from death and will cover a multitude of sins" (5:20). This does not mean that the soul-winner covers his own sins by his exercise in evangelism. The sins covered are those of the restored believer. Sometimes, the word "cover" is translated *atonement*. When a sinner is saved, God covers the sinner with Christ's righteousness. Freely, fully, finally, and forever one's sins are covered. James, Jesus' brother, had denied the lordship of his own half brother. Jesus had restored him. James's remarkable, inspired letter resulted from the restoration.

Lessons for Life from James 5:7-20

Identify the areas in your life where you most lack the patient ability to persevere steadfastly.—You may lack the ability to persevere at home with the family, at work with a task, or at church with a ministry assignment. Keep a calendar of your progress with such commitments and go on in steadfast endurance through days of difficulty.

Determine not to take part or to stop taking part in the "grumblers club" at your church.—Trivia is traumatizing many Baptist churches. Trivia really is not trivial. Determine that you will speak a positive word and leave the negative to those who always are ready to speak it.

Take James's advice and carefully study the life of a prophet.—

Compare and contrast his reactions to life's trials with your reactions.

Inventory how you face life's suffering.—Does it make you bitter or better? Do you meet it with prayer?

Experience a resurgence of interest in praising God.—Commit a time in your daily devotion this week totally to praising God. Use the Bible's praise psalms, praise hymns, and good religious poetry to express your praise to God.

Consider your role in your church's ministry to the sick.—Is prayer for the sick a regular part of your life?

1. Robert S. Eliot and Dennis L. Breo, *Is It Worth Dying For?* (New York: Bantam Books, 1984), pp. 38-54.

2. From *The New English Bible.* Copyright © The Delegates of the Oxford University Press and the Syndics of the Cambridge University Press, 1961, 1970. Reprinted by permission.

3. Roy Hosler, "Ironnism," *Runner's World*, Jan., 1984, p. 64.

4. "How Firm a Foundation," from John F. Wade's *Cantus Diversi*, 1751.

5. William Barclay, *The Letters of James and Peter*, (Philadelphia: Westminster Press, 1960), p. 152.

6. R. J. Knowling, *The Epistle of St. James* (London: Methuen and Company, 1904), p. 137.

7. Curtis Vaughan, *James: A Study Guide* (Grand Rapids, Mich.: Zondervan Pub. House, 1969), 116.

8. W. A. Criswell, *Expository Sermons on the Epistle of James* (Grand Rapids, Mich.: Zondervan Pub. House, 1975), p. 109.

9. John Wilkinson, "Healing in the Epistle of James," *Scottish Journal of Theology*, August, 1971, pp. 338-39.

10. James Hardy Ropes, *A Critical and Exegetical Commentary on the Epistle of St. James* (Edinburgh: T & T Clark, 1954), pp. 308-309.

11. Sophie Laws, *A Commentary on the Epistle of James* (New York: Harper & Row, Publishers, 1980), p. 229.

12. James I. Packer, "Poor Health May Be the Best Remedy," *Christianity Today*, 21, May, 1982, p. 15.

Personal Learning Activities

1. In James 5:7, the word translated "patience" means (choose the correct answers from the list):

____(1) Tolerance. ____(3) Long-tempered.

____(2) Endurance. ____(4) Passive waiting.

2. James used _____, _____, and _____
   as examples of patience. (Select the proper responses from the
   list.)
   (1) An athlete   (3) The prophets
   (2) A farmer   (4) Job
3. James advised his readers to _____ in bad days and to
   _____ in good days. (Choose the correct answers from the
   list.)
   (1) Try harder   (3) Pray   (5) Indulge
   (2) Quit   (4) Relax   (6) Praise
4. James used _____ as an example of the power of a righteous person's prayer. (Select the correct response from the list.)
   (1) Abraham   (3) Elijah
   (2) Paul   (4) Moses

Answers:

1. (2),(3); 2. (2),(3),(4); 3. (3),(6); 4. (3).

The Church Study Course

The Church Study Course consists of a variety of short-term credit courses for adults and youth and noncredit foundational units for children and preschoolers. The materials are for use in addition to the study and training curriculums made available to the churches on an ongoing basis.

Study courses and foundational units are organized into a system that is promoted by the Sunday School Board, 127 Ninth Avenue, North, Nashville, Tennessee 37234; by the Woman's Missionary Union, Highway 280, East, 100 Missionary Ridge, Birmingham, Alabama 35243-2798; by the Brotherhood Commission, 1548 Poplar Avenue, Memphis, Tennessee 38104; and by the respective departments of the state conventions affiliated with the Southern Baptist Convention.

Study course materials are flexible enough to be adapted to the needs of any Baptist church. The resources are published in several different formats—textbooks of various sizes, workbooks, and kits. Each item contains a brief explanation of the Church Study Course and information on requesting credit. Additional information and interpretation are available from the participating agencies.

Types of Study and Credit

Adults and youth can earn study course credit through individual or group study. Teachers of courses or of foundational units also are eligible to receive credit.

1. Class Experience.—Group involvement with course material for the designated number of hours for the particular course and reading the textbook. A person who is absent from one or more sessions must complete the "Personal Learning Activities" or other requirements for the course.
2. Individual Study.—Reading, viewing, or listening to course material and completing the specified requirements for the course.
3. Lesson Course Study.—Parallel use of designated study

course material during the study of selected units in Church Program Organization periodical curriculum units. Guidance for this means of credit is in the selected periodical.

4. Institutional Study.—Parallel use of designated study course material during regular courses at educational institutions, including Seminary Extension Department courses. Guidance for this means of credit is provided by the teacher.

Credit is awarded for the successful completion of a course of study. This credit is granted by the Church Study Course Awards Office, 127 Ninth Avenue, North, Nashville, Tennessee 37234, for the participating agencies. Form 725 (available free) is recommended for use in requesting credit.

A permanent record of courses and diplomas will be maintained by the Awards Office. Twice each year, up-to-date reports called "transcripts" will be sent to churches to distribute to members who take part in the Church Study Course. Each transcript will list courses and diplomas that participants have completed and will show progress toward diplomas that are being sought. The transcript will show which courses are needed to complete diploma requirements. A diploma will be issued automatically when the final requirement is met.

Detailed information about the Church Study Course system of credits, diplomas, and record keeping is available from the participating agencies. Study course materials, supplementary teaching or learning aids, and forms for record keeping may be ordered from Baptist Book Stores.

The Church Study Course Curriculum

Credit is granted on those courses listed in the current copy of the *Church Services and Materials Catalog* and the *Church Study Course Catalog*. When selecting courses or foundational units, check the current catalogs to determine what study course materials are valid.

How to Request Credit
for This Course

This book is designed for a course in the subject area Bible Studies.

This course is designed for 5 hours of group study. Credit is awarded for satisfactory class experience with the study material for the minimum number of hours which includes reading the textbook. A person who is absent from one or more sessions must complete the "Personal Learning Activities" or other requirements for the materials missed.

Credit also is allowed for use of this material in individual study and in institutional study, if so designated.

The following requirements must be met for credit:
1. Read the book *James: Faith Works!*
2. Attend at least 5 hours of class study or complete all "Personal Learning Activities" (see end of each chapter). Class members who are absent from one or more class sessions must complete "Personal Learning Activities" on chapters missed. In such a case, they must turn in their papers by the date the teacher sets, usually within ten days following the last class.

Credit in this course may be earned through individual study. The requirements for such credit are:
1. Read the book.
2. Complete the "Personal Learning Activities" on the chapters.

Credit in this course may be earned through study in an educational institution, if so designated by a teacher. The requirements are:
1. Read the book.
2. Fulfill the requirements of the course taught at the institution.

After the course is completed, the teacher, the study course records librarian, the learner, or any person designated by the church should complete Form 725 ("Church Study Course Enrollment/Credit Request") and send it to the Awards Office, 127 Ninth

Avenue, North, Nashville, Tennessee 37234. In the back of this book the reader will find a form which may be cut out, filled in, and sent to the Awards Office.

CHURCH STUDY COURSE
ENROLLMENT/CREDIT REQUEST (FORM-725)

PERSONAL CSC NUMBER (If Known)

INSTRUCTIONS:

1. Please PRINT or TYPE.
2. COURSE CREDIT REQUEST—Requirements must be met. Use exact title.
3. ENROLLMENT IN DIPLOMA PLANS—Enter selected diploma title to enroll.
4. For additional information see the Church Study Course Catalog.
5. Duplicate additional forms as needed. Free forms are available from the Awards Office and State Conventions.

TYPE OF REQUEST: (Check all that apply)

☐ Course Credit
☐ Enrollment in Diploma Plan

☐ Address Change
☐ Name Change
☐ Church Change

REQUEST FOR

☐ Mr. ☐ Miss
☐ Mrs.

DATE OF BIRTH ⬆

	Month	Day	Year

Name (First, MI, Last)

Street, Route, or P.O. Box

City, State, Zip Code

ENROLLMENT IN DIPLOMA PLANS

If you have not previously indicated a diploma(s) you wish to earn, or you are beginning work on a new one(s), select and enter the diploma title from the current Church Study Course Catalog. Select one that relates to your leadership responsibility or interest. When all requirements have been met, the diploma will be automatically mailed to your church. No charge will be made for enrollment or diplomas.

➤

Title of diploma	Age group or area
1.	➤
Title of diploma	Age group or area
2.	
Signature of Pastor, Teacher, or Study Leader	Date

CHURCH

Church Name

Mailing Address

City, State, Zip Code

COURSE CREDIT REQUEST

Course No	Use exact title
04111	1. James: Faith Works!
Course No	Use exact title
	2.
Course No	Use exact title
	3.
Course No	Use exact title
	4.
Course No	Use exact title
	5.

MAIL THIS REQUEST TO ⬆

CHURCH STUDY COURSE AWARDS OFFICE
RESEARCH SERVICES DEPARTMENT
127 NINTH AVENUE, NORTH
NASHVILLE, TENNESSEE 37234

FORM-725 (Rev. 7-83)